MW01093666

Ole Miss

Daily Devotions for Die-Hard Kids

Rebels

Ole Miss

TO PARENTS/GUARDIANS FROM THE AUTHOR

DAILY DEVOTIONS FOR DIE-HARD KIDS is an adaptation of our DAILY DEVOTIONS FOR DIE-HARD FANS series. It is suggested for children ages 6 to 12, but that guideline is, of course, flexible. Only the parents or other adults can appraise the spiritual maturity of their children.

The devotions are written with the idea that a parent or adult will join the children to act as a mentor and spiritual guide for each devotion and the discussion that may ensue. The devotions seek to engage the child by capitalizing on his or her interest in the particular collegiate team the family follows. The interest in college sports is thus an oblique and somewhat tricky way, if you will, to lead your children to reading the Bible and learning about God, Jesus, and faith.

Each devotion contains a short Bible reading (except for occasional longer stories that must be read in their entirety), a paraphrase of the most pertinent scripture verse, a true Ole Miss sports story, and a theological discussion that ties everything together through a common theme. The devotion then concludes with a suggested activity that is based on the theme of the day. I tie each day's theological message to a child's life by referring to such aspects as school, household chores, video games, and relations with parents, siblings, and teachers, etc.

The devotions are intended to be fun for both the adult and the child, but they are also intended to be attempts to spark interest in quite serious matters of faith and living a godly life. A point of emphasis throughout the book is to impress upon the child that faith is not just for the times when the family gathers for formal worship in a particular structure, but rather is for every moment of every day wherever he or she may be.

Our children are under attack by the secular world as never before. It is a time fraught with danger for the innocence and the faith of our most precious family members. I pray that this book will provide your children with a better understanding of what it means to be a Christian. I also pray that this book will help lay the foundation for what will be a lifelong journey of faith for your children. May God bless you and your family.

ED MCMINN

Rebels

Daily Devotions for Die-Hard Kids: Ole Miss Rebels
© 2016 Ed McMinn; Extra Point Publishers; P.O. Box 871; Perry GA 31069

Manufactured in the United States of America.
To order books or for more information, visit us at www.die-hardfans.com
Cover design by John Powell and Slynn McMinn;
Interior design by Slynn McMinn

DAILY DEVOTIONS FOR DIE-HARD FANS

ACC
CLEMSON TIGERS
DUKE BLUE DEVILS
FSU SEMINOLES
GA. TECH YELLOW JACKETS
NORTH CAROLINA TAR HEELS
NC STATE WOLFPACK
NOTRE DAME FIGHTING IRISH
VIRGINIA CAVALIERS
VIRGINIA TECH HOKIES

BIG 12
BAYLOR BEARS
OKLAHOMA SOONERS
OKLAHOMA STATE COWBOYS
TCU HORNED FROGS
TEXAS LONGHORNS
TEXAS TECH RED RAIDERS
WEST VIRGINIA MOUNTAINEERS

BIG 10
MICHIGAN WOLVERINES
NEBRASKA CORNHUSKERS
OHIO STATE BUCKEYES
PENN STATE NITTANY LIONS

SEC
ALABAMA CRIMSON TIDE
MORE ALABAMA CRIMSON TIDE
ARKANSAS RAZORBACKS
AUBURN TIGERS
MORE AUBURN TIGERS
FLORIDA GATORS
GEORGIA BULLDOGS
MORE GEORGIA BULLDOGS
KENTUCKY WILDCATS
LSU TIGERS
MISSISSIPPI STATE BULLDOGS
MISSOURI TIGERS
OLE MISS REBELS
SOUTH CAROLINA GAMECOCKS
MORE S. CAROLINA GAMECOCKS
TEXAS A&M AGGIES
TENNESSEE VOLUNTEERS

NASCAR

DAILY DEVOTIONS FOR DIE-HARD KIDS

ALABAMA CRIMSON TIDE; BAYLOR BEARS; AUBURN TIGERS;
GEORGIA BULLDOGS; LSU TIGERS MISS. STATE BULLDOGS;
OLE MISS REBELS; TEXAS LONGHORNS; TEXAS A&M AGGIES

IN THE BEGINNING

Read Genesis 1:1; 2:1-3.

In the beginning, God created the heavens and the earth.

When a bunch of young Baptists piled off a train, they were met by a bunch of laughing people from Mississippi. It was 1893, and football at Ole Miss had begun.

For six weeks, a young professor of Latin and Greek had led sixteen students in practicing for the school's first-ever football game. He taught them the basics. He also had the boys promise not to smoke or to drink coffee or tea and to be in bed by 10 each night.

Some Oxford folks collected money to buy some cheap uniforms for the players. They had to come up with their own shoes and had to pay their own medical bills if they got hurt. The professor chose Harvard red and Yale blue as the team colors.

Rebels

The first opponent was Southwestern Baptist University. A big crowd met them at the train station and rode them around town in carriages pulled by horses. Before kickoff, the boys sat around and talked things over.

Ole Miss won the game 56-0. "Every man did his duty," the professor wrote about that game that began football at Ole Miss.

Beginnings are important, but how we use those beginnings is even more important. You get a new beginning in your life every time the sun comes up and brings you a new day.

Have you ever thought that every morning is a gift from God? Well, it is. This present of a new day shows God's love for you. Each new day is full of promise. You can use it to make some wrong things right and to do some good.

How you use your new day is up to you. You should just make sure you walk with God all day long.

Try starting each morning by thanking God for the day and asking him to protect and lead you all day long.

STRANGE BUT TRUE

Read Philippians 2:5-11.

Jesus is God, but he became a servant and died on a cross.

It's strange but it's true: Ole Miss once had a football game decided by a field goal that was good — and then was no good.

Miss. State led the 1983 Egg Bowl 23-7 at the end of the third quarter. But then came one of the strangest comebacks in football history.

The Bulldogs fumbled twice and threw an interception. The Rebels turned all those mistakes into points. The strange part is that they scored 17 points with only 52 yards of offense, which isn't very much. They led 24-23.

That wasn't as strange as the game's end. With 24 seconds left, the Bulldogs tried a field goal to win it. One writer said the kick "went straight and long and over the crossbar, and

Rebels

State fans went wild." They thought State had won. That's not how it went, though.

As the ball was in the air, a sudden gust of wind estimated at 40 mph incredibly pushed the ball back. It fell short of the crossbar, and now Ole Miss fans went nuts. 24-23 Rebels.

It was called the only field goal ever celebrated by both fans. Isn't that strange?

A lot of things about life are strange. Isn't it strange that you can't eat all the sugar you want to? Isn't it strange that you can't play all the time when everybody knows that's what kids are good at?

God's kind of strange, too, isn't he? He's the ruler of all the universe; he can do anything he wants to. And so he let himself be killed by a bunch of men who nailed him to two pieces of wood. Isn't that downright weird?

And why did God do it? That's strange, too. He did it because he loves you so much. In the person of Jesus, God died so you can be his friend.

List five things about God that are strange. Tell why they're strange.

GROWING PAINS

Read Mark 4:30-32.

God's kingdom is like a tiny mustard seed that grows into the largest garden plant of all.

To talk about growing in your life means you are getting better at something. A really good basketball player went to Oxford to grow — but it wasn't just on the court.

Todd Abernethy finished his career at Ole Miss with the 2006-07 season. He is sixth all-time in the Rebels' record book with 158 career three-pointers. He scored more than 1,000 points.

Abernethy was from Indiana. He came to Ole Miss even though he knew nothing about Oxford. And head coach Rod Barnes had never seen him play.

How in the world? All it took was one phone

call. As they talked, the two discovered they shared a deep, abiding faith in Jesus Christ.

That was good enough for Abernethy. He wanted a place where he could grow not just as a basketball player but also as a Christian. Ole Miss was the place.

You will learn — if you haven't already — that most really good things in life take time to grow. It takes years for you to grow into a man or a woman. It takes twelve years of school before you're ready to go to Ole Miss.

Your faith life, too, must grow over time. You look at some grown-ups, and they seem to know the whole Bible. They're like saints.

Well, those saints didn't just pop out of a pea hull like that. They have spent years studying, praying, and growing in their faith.

It's OK for you to start small in your faith. Faith is a lifelong trip; you just keep moving on to bigger and better things in God.

Ask your pastor or Sunday school teacher to tell you his/her story about how his/her faith has grown.

Ole Miss

TOP SECRET

Read Romans 2:1-4, 16.

One day, God will appoint Jesus to judge everyone's secret thoughts.

The Ole Miss football program was in such bad shape in 1946 that the team didn't even have any uniforms to play in. But the team had a big secret that would change everything.

World War II took the Rebels' best players and left the program in a big mess. The new head coach in 1946 had to borrow some old uniforms from Alabama to begin the season against Kentucky. Most of the pants didn't fit. Some of them were so small that they looked like shorts on the Ole Miss players.

The team limped to a pitiful 2-7 record, and the head coach left to take a job at Alabama.

But that coaching staff in 1946 had a secret. He was a little-known coach who had come to Ole Miss after serving in the U.S. Navy during the war. Everybody quickly came to call this big Texan "the backbone of the staff." One player said, "At halftime . . . he could go to the blackboard and help. . . . The others just jumped up and down and cussed."

That secret was Johnny Vaught, the greatest head football coach in Ole Miss history.

You probably have some secrets you keep from certain people. Do you tell your sisters and brothers everything? How about your mom and dad? Maybe there's a girl or a boy at school or at church that you really like but you haven't told anyone.

You can keep some secrets from the world. You must never think, though, that you can keep a secret from God. God knows everything about you. He knows all the bad things you say, do, or think and all the good things.

But here's something that's not a secret: No matter what God knows about you, he still loves you. Enough to die for you on a cross.

Does it make you feel good or bad that God knows all your secrets? Why?

Ole Miss

ON CALL

Read 1 Samuel 3:1-10.

Samuel said, "Speak, Lord. I'm listening."

What do you do if a whole bunch of your starting players can't play? If you're Ole Miss, you answer the call and win anyway.

Against Auburn in 2003, the Rebel sideline began to look like a little hospital for great big people. Three offensive linemen got hurt, joining other Rebs on the injured list. Stacy Andrews, who had never played football before the season, went in at right tackle. That's how bad it was.

Andrews was just one of a list of second- and third-team guys who had to play because there wasn't anybody else. Quarterback Eli Manning had to get with the linemen on the sideline to explain to them what they were supposed to do on some plays.

Rebels

With all those new players on the field, the Rebs went 81 yards in nine plays and scored a touchdown late in the game. Those backups answered the call right on to a 24-20 win.

You may have answered the call when a coach needed you to play a new position in a game. Or when your teacher calls on you to answer a question.

Did you know God, too, is calling you? God wants you to do something for him with your life. That sounds scary, doesn't it?

But answering God's call doesn't mean you have to be a preacher or a Sunday school teacher. Or be a missionary in some way-off place where they never heard of fried chicken or the Ole Miss Rebels.

God calls you to serve him right where you are. At school. At home. On the playground. You answer God's call when you do everything for his glory and not your own.

Talk and pray with your parents about the call God might be placing on your life and how you can answer it.

GOOD ADVICE

Read Isaiah 9:6-7.

A son will be given to us, and he will be called Wonderful Adviser.

A father found his son crying on his bed and gave him some advice. The son became an Ole Miss legend.

Why was the boy crying? "I don't know if I can make it," he told his dad. He had wanted his whole life to play quarterback for Ole Miss, but he wasn't sure he was good enough. The competition at Ole Miss was too tough.

So the dad stepped in with some advice. He told his son not worry about the other players. "They wouldn't want you at Ole Miss if they didn't think you can play," he said. Then he added, "If you have made up your mind that's where you want to go, you shouldn't change it."

The son followed his dad's advice and stuck

Rebels

by his decision to play for the Rebels.

The year was 1966. That talented youngster who needed some advice was Archie Manning, still considered by many to be the greatest player in Ole Miss history.

"All I needed was my dad to say something," he later said. "That made up my mind."

Just about everybody tells you what to do. Your parents, your teachers, your coaches — they all order you around.

That's different from advice. You may get advice from your friends or classmates, from older kids or your brothers or sisters. They don't tell you what to do, but they may say you should dress, act, or talk a certain way.

The problem is you don't really know whether their advice is good or bad. Do you have a place that always gives you good advice?

Yes, you do. It's called the Bible. In it, God advises you on how you are to live. God's advice is always good; it will never hurt you.

Ask a parent for advice about how to handle a problem you have at school.

Ole Miss

IN GOD'S OWN TIME

Read James 5:7-11.

Be patient, for the Lord is coming.

The greatest softball player in Ole Miss history had to learn something new her senior year: patience.

Playing from 2007-10, Lauren Grill was the first Rebel softball player ever to be named first team All-America. She set a whole bunch of school records and was the first Rebel to be named All-SEC three times.

But before her senior season, Grill decided she needed to make a change in the way she hit. Why in the world would she do that?

Her batting average her junior year had been her lowest ever, and she knew why. She was swinging at too many pitches that were not strikes. She decided to be patient when she batted. She would take the walks if the pitchers gave them to her.

Rebels

So Grill became a more patient hitter. As a result, she had a great senior season. She led the team with a .444 batting average. She also led the squad in home runs, RBIs, and slugging percentage. Her patience let her get on base more than half the time, an incredible achievement.

Patience means you can wait for something without getting upset. Can you wait to grow up? Can you wait for the weekend when you can play instead of having to go to school? And have you ever prayed for something and asked God to give it to you right away?

People do that a lot, get impatient with God. But God likes you to be patient, just as he likes you to be gentle and kind. The truth is that God moves in his own time, at his own pace. God knows what he is doing. He is in control, and his will shall be done.

Prayer shows you depend on God. Patience shows you trust God.

Get something you like to eat and a watch. Sit down. Wait five minutes by the watch before you chow down.

ONE TOUGH COOKIE

Read 2 Corinthians 11:23-28.

Besides everything else, every day I worry about the churches.

Ole Miss fans will long remember Bo Wallace as one tough football player.

A quarterback, Wallace is the school's all-time offense leader. He passed Eli Manning. The senior quarterback sprained his ankle in the Arkansas game the week before the 2014 Egg Bowl. He was hurt, but there was no way he was going to miss the game. Rebel head coach Hugh Freeze said the coaches would have had to chain the injured player to a chair to keep him out of the game.

Wallace never complained as he got ready to play Miss. State, no matter how much he hurt. He taped his ankle up and took some pain medication. Then he went out and passed for 296 yards in the big 31-17 defeat of the fourth-ranked Bulldogs.

But he did something nobody was expecting. Despite that gimpy ankle, he scored on a 1-yard run. Talk about tough! Wallace's touchdown gave the Rebs a 7-3 halftime lead.

You don't have to be an Ole Miss football player to be tough, do you? It's tough to get up every morning and get to school on time. It's tough to get all your homework done.

It's also tough to be faithful. Nobody today will beat you up for believing in Jesus as they did Paul. But some people you meet — maybe your classmates — may make fun of you for being a Christian. Or they will do things that are wrong and want you to do them, too.

You have to be tough every day to live the way God wants you to. You stay spiritually fit every day by reading your Bible, praying, and by helping and loving others. Living that way every day makes you tough in God's eyes.

Promise God you'll stay tough all month by reading your Bible, praying, and helping someone else every day. Do it.

A SECOND CHANCE

Read Acts 9:1-6, 13-15.

God said, "I have chosen Paul to work for me."

The Rebels once got a second chance they didn't want or need. The result was a wild ending to a game and a big old fuss.

The Rebels of 1960 won the national title. One of their roughest game was against the Arkansas Razorbacks.

With three seconds left in the game, senior Allen Green hit a field goal for a 10-7 Rebel win. Fans started celebrating. Not so fast, football breath! One referee had blown the play dead because of the crowd noise. The Rebels would have to kick the field goal a second time.

Green's kick started out perfectly — and then hooked to the left as it neared the goalposts. The ref who had stopped play earlier raised his arms straight up: The kick was good.

Rebels

Almost everyone in the whole state of Arkansas disagreed. Some Arkansas players said they went into the dressing room thinking the game had ended in a tie.

The ref said about the kick, "If it hadn't been good, I wouldn't have called it good."

Paul was an evil man, persecuting and killing Christians, until he met Jesus. Then his life changed forever. Like Paul, you need a second chance now and then. Like taking a test over. Or getting another at-bat after you've struck out in a softball or a baseball game.

Here's something really cool. With God, you always get a second chance. God will never, ever give up on you. He will always give you another chance when you do wrong. Nothing you can do will make God stop loving you.

You just have to go to him and ask for his forgiveness. Then you get a second chance. Every time.

Think about a time you made a mistake. If you got a second chance, what would you do differently?

THE PROPHET

Read Isaiah 53:6-9.

He went like a lamb to the slaughter and said not a word.

"We're going to win them all." Ole Miss halfback and defensive back Billy Kinard turned out to be a pretty good prophet.

Kinard made his bold prediction at a strange time. The Rebels had won the SEC in 1954 behind a defense that was the best in the country. They were favored to win it again in 1955. But then Kentucky upset them 21-14 in the second game of the season.

About two hundred disappointed but faithful fans met the team bus when it arrived on campus after the loss. Walking through the crowd, Kinard raised his fist and delivered his prophecy: "We're going to win them all!"

It was pretty far-fetched. But guess what? Billy Kinard was right on. The Rebs won eight straight games to finish the season 9-1. They became the third team in history to win back-to-back SEC championships.

They then went to the Cotton Bowl in Dallas, Texas, and nipped TCU 14-13. It was the first-ever win in a major bowl game for the Rebels.

So, Ole Miss did indeed win them all.

In the Old Testament, you read a lot about God's prophets. Isaiah was one. Did those guys walk around predicting the future like some scary palm reader? Not really.

Instead, they delivered a word that God had given them. Sometimes — as when Isaiah spoke of Jesus' suffering and death — that involved the future. But typically, the prophets told the people what God wanted them to do and how God said they should live.

Where is your prophet? How can you find out what God wants you to do? You read the Bible and you pray. It's all right there for you.

Write down five predictions (like your next test grade). Check them later to see how many you got right.

Ole Miss

GOOD-BYE

Read John 13:33-36.

Jesus told Peter, "Where I am going, you can't follow now."

The Rebels had such a good time saying good-bye they didn't want to leave.

On Jan. 1, 2009, the Cotton Bowl game was played in the stadium of the same name for the 73rd and final time. The Rebels were there to help say good-bye to the old building.

First-year Ole Miss head coach Houston Nutt grew up in Arkansas with the Cotton Bowl on New Year's Day. "Mom had black-eyed peas going and cornbread while we were getting ready to watch the Cotton Bowl," he recalled.

Ole Miss took on a favored Texas Tech team and ate them alive. The Rebels rolled up 515 yards worth of offense behind 292 yards passing from quarterback Jevan Snead.

When the final score of 47-34 was on the

board and the clock had ticked down to zero, the Rebel players didn't want to say good-bye. They did backflips at midfield, made a sprint to the student section, and dashed around on the field carrying oversized flags.

Even though you're a youngster, you have probably known good-byes — and they hurt. Maybe your best friend moved away. Maybe you moved away and had to tell a whole lot of your friends and buddies good-bye. It's sad to stand and wave while your grandparents drive off on their way home after a visit.

Jesus knows just how you feel. He always had his friends around him, but it came time for him to tell them good-bye. He was going away; he would leave them.

But Jesus wasn't just moving across the county line. He was about to finish his mission on Earth. He would provide a way so that none of us would ever have to say good-bye again.

List some people you have said good-bye to. Get their addresses from a parent and write them a note.

CHEERS

Read Matthew 21:6-11.

Some people ran ahead of Jesus, and some followed him. They all shouted.

The Ole Miss students had a favorite cheer a long time ago in 1910. You better not count on it coming back anytime soon.

For the first time ever, the school had a full-time athletic director in 1910. The football season that year put up the best record the school had ever had. That team of '10 went 7-1; the only loss was 9-2 to Vanderbilt. Vandy, by the way, was the only team to score on the Rebels the whole season.

Things were a lot different back then. For instance, officials from what would become Mississippi State asked the Rebel head coach to serve as a ref for one of its games.

And the students' favorite cheer? It went

like this: "Boomalacka, boomalacka, wow, wow, wow; chickalack, chickalack, chow, chow, chow; boomalack, chickalack, way, who, wah; Mississippi, Mississippi, rah, rah, rah!

Hey, you go to school in the morning. You do your homework and your chores. You go to church. You remember to say "Yes, sir" and "Yes ma'am" — most of the time.

Overall, you're a pretty good kid, but nobody cheers for you. No announcer calls your name. Nobody hollers "Boomalacka" or "Chickalack" at you when you pass by.

That's okay. Think what happened to Jesus. A crowd went wild cheering for him when he entered Jerusalem. They threw their clothes on the ground and tore branches off trees. Five days later, the crowd shouted again. Only this time they screamed for Jesus to be killed.

You just remember that you have a personal cheerleader who will never stop pulling for you.

That cheerleader is God.

At a mirror, shout the "Boomalacka" cheer real loud for God three times.

Ole Miss

IN A WORD

Read Matthew 12:33-37.

A good man says good things, but an evil man speaks evil words.

Charley Conerly was one of football's greatest quarterbacks. He didn't talk too much; he just let his actions speak for him.

For a long time, Conerly had a sign on his desk that said, "Speak softly and tenderly for tomorrow you may have to eat your words." He meant it because while he did a lot, he said very little.

Some folks said the horrors he saw in World War II forged his quiet manner. Others said it was because of all the cane he raised when he was growing up. He came to see that a real man leads by example and not by words.

Someone once asked him how he got the timing to throw a football the way he did. He said he believed "God gives everybody some talent. He gave it to me and I'd better use it the best way I can."

He did. Conerly was All-SEC for the Rebels in 1946. He was also the team's punter. As a senior in 1947, Conerly was an All-American. He went on to an All-Pro career in the NFL and never did say too much about any of it.

Words can hurt. When somebody at school says ugly things to you or calls you a name, it hurts your feelings, doesn't it?

Words have power for good or for bad. The words you speak at school or on the ballfield can make other kids cry. But they can also make your friends feel good and smile.

Don't ever make the mistake of thinking what you say doesn't matter. Speaking the Word of God was the only way Jesus had of getting his message to others. Look what he managed to do.

Watch what you say; others sure will.

With a parent, listen to three songs on a cell phone. Decide if what they say is good or bad. Promise you will listen only to music with good words.

GREAT EXPECTATIONS

Read John 1:43-49.

Nathanael asked, "Nazareth! Can anything good come from there?"

Maggie McFerrin didn't expect to make the Ole Miss women's basketball team. She sure didn't expect to play. So much for that.

In high school, McFerrin was all-state in basketball, track, and cross country. She gave up on sports, though, when she went to Ole Miss in 2009. She figured she wasn't good enough to play in the SEC. She spent the year playing basketball as much as she could with friends and buddies. But then she got the itch again.

Then head coach Renee Ladner held tryouts. McFerrin didn't know it, but some of the varsity players had seen her play. They told the head coach how good she was; she made the team.

That was all McFerrin expected. She didn't think she'd ever play. So when Ladner told her to go in during a game, she thought, "Oh, my gosh. I'm about to go in!"

Later in the 2010-11 season, a starter was injured, and this sophomore who didn't expect to make the team became a part-time starter. She was in the lineup for the next two seasons.

Everybody expects a lot of stuff from you, don't they? Your parents expect you to mind your manners and behave. They expect you to do your chores, like keep your room clean. They expect you to make good grades.

Your teachers expect you to sit down and be quiet in class. They expect you to do all your class work and your homework.

Have you ever thought that God expects a lot from you, too? Nathanael didn't expect anything good to come from Nazareth, but it did. And God expects something good to come from you, too.

God expects you to live like Jesus, and that is more important than anything else.

Name some things God expects from you. How are you doing?

DRY RUN

Read 1 Kings 16:29-30; 17:1; 18:1.

Elijah told Ahab, "There won't be any rain for the next few years."

The Ole Miss football team was having a big dry spell. The drought ended with a thrilling, last-minute win.

In 1983, the Rebels hadn't been to a bowl game in twelve seasons. They hadn't won an SEC game in almost two seasons. So the Vanderbilt Commodores were favored when they came to Oxford on Oct. 22.

Ole Miss led 21-14 with 1:37 left but had a field goal blocked. With only 38 ticks on the clock, Vandy sat at the Rebel 45.

Then to the horror of the home crowd, Vandy dropped a bomb to the tight end all the way to the Ole Miss 1-yard line. A quick pass out of bounds stopped the clock with 17 seconds left. Vanderbilt then got a penalty that moved the ball back to the 6.

The long dry run ended when cornerback Eric Truitt made a dramatic, game-saving interception in the end zone. The Rebs went on to beat LSU, Tennessee, and Miss. State back-to-back. The bowl drought ended, too.

If you live in the South, you know a little something about drought, don't you? It gets really hot down here, and sometimes in the summer you probably don't get a whole lot of rain in your hometown.

The sun bakes everything, including the concrete that gets so hot it burns your feet. Ever seen a truck with "Wash Me" written on the back windshield? Kinda funny, isn't it?

God put in you a physical thirst for water to keep you alive. But he also put a spiritual thirst in you. Without God, we are like a dried-up pond. There's no life, only death.

There's only one fountain to go to and drink all you want of the true water of life: Jesus.

Fill an empty water bottle with sand to remind you how a soul looks without God: all dried up and dead.

Ole Miss

HUGS AND KISSES

Read John 15:9-14.

Jesus said, "I have loved you. Now remain in my love."

The Ole Miss head football coach once got hugged by players from both teams after a game.

The Rebels had lost four straight to Arkansas when they met in 2008. That season had a big difference, though. The first-year Ole Miss head coach was Houston Nutt. He had been the Arkansas coach for all four of those losses.

After ten seasons as the boss of the Razorbacks, Nutt took over in Oxford in 2008. This time he was the enemy when he went back to Arkansas for the game. "It was very hard," Nutt admitted.

A late field goal sent the Rebels to a 23-21 win, and the Arkansas fans didn't like it at all. One threw an empty water cup at Nutt, and another threw a cup of ice his way. Boos rolled down from the stands.

Not from the Arkansas players, though. Nutt had recruited them, had been in their homes. They were still his boys even though they were on the other sideline. Many of them greeted their old coach with smiles and big hugs.

A hug is a sign of affection. When you hug someone, you're showing them you care for them. It doesn't just make them feel good; it makes you feel good, too.

A hug is also a symbol. When you hold someone close, it says how closely you hold them in your heart.

The greatest hugger of all is God. Through Jesus, God tries to pull us closer to him because he loves us. A good hug takes two, so God always wants us to hug him back.

We do that by loving Jesus. To love Jesus is to hug God — and that feels mighty good.

Think of some folks you'd like to give a great big hug to and then do it the next time you see them.

SIZE MATTERS

Read Luke 19:1-10.

Zacchaeus wanted to see Jesus, but he was so short, he had to climb a tree.

The new Rebel head coach took one look at his players and said if that was as big as they got, he was going back to Georgia.

Harry Mehre came to Oxford in 1938 after being let go at UGA. Over the next eight seasons, he became the winningest coach in Ole Miss history to that time.

His first day on the job, he met two of his players, Junie Hovious and Billy Sam. Both students weighed a whopping 135 pounds and were said to be "only slightly larger than a minute." That meeting led the new coach to think about getting on a train back to Georgia.

But size isn't everything, as Mehre learned. Finally weighing 150 pounds, Hovious was the team's star running back for three seasons. He was All-SEC three times and was later the Rebel golf coach for 25 years. Sam lettered three years at right halfback. Both players are members of the school's hall of fame.

Everybody seems to think bigger is better. Bigger houses, bigger burgers. You even super-size your fries. You just can't wait to grow up some so you can be taller and bigger, can you?

But, you know, size didn't matter to Jesus. One time, salvation came to the house of a bad man who was so short he had to climb a tree to see Jesus. Zacchaeus was a big shot because he was rich, but that didn't matter to Jesus either. Zacchaeus was saved because he was sorry for all the wrong things he had done, and he changed his life as a result.

The same is true for you. What matters to Jesus is the size of your heart, the one you give to him.

***Look at some of your old pictures.
Have you grown much?
Have you grown in your love for Jesus?***

IT'S IMPOSSIBLE!

Read Matthew 19:23-26.

With God, all things are possible.

An Ole Miss lineman once made a play a sportswriter said was impossible.

The Rebels of 1963 won the SEC title. They went 7-0-2 with a defense that was the best in the country.

The highlight of the season was a 37-3 romp over LSU. The highlight of that big win was a play pulled off by sophomore guard Stan Hindman. Ole Miss punted with a 23-3 lead. The LSU return man caught the ball and broke into the clear with a lot of grass in front of him.

He was LSU's fastest player while Hindman was a lineman. There was no way he could get close enough to read the runner's jersey number, let alone tackle him.

But Hindman did the impossible: He ran the LSU player down, made the tackle, and saved a touchdown. LSU couldn't score and never got close to the Rebel goal line again.

Ole Miss coasted to a big win thanks in part to an "impossible" play."

Some things in life are just impossible. You will never turn into a cat, a TV set, or a rock. Next week won't have five days. The sun won't rise in the west tomorrow morning. You can never run cross-country or get to Heaven.

Whoa, wait just a minute! What about those last two? Are they impossible? Not with Jesus helping you along the way, they're not.

Your faith and the inspiration it can give you make all things possible for you. Things like playing a sport or singing in church. And when you believe in Jesus as your savior, you have reservations in Heaven.

Even as a kid or a young person, your faith means you live each day believing you can do whatever you set your mind to if you rely on God and work hard for it. Get on it!

List three things that are impossible. List three that with God's help you can do.

Ole Miss

I TOLD YOU SO

Read Matthew 24:30-35.

Jesus will come on the clouds in power and glory.

Before one of the biggest basketball games in Rebel history, the head coach told his players what to say after they won.

The Rebs of 1996-97 went 20-9. It was the program's first 20-win season in almost sixty years. They won the SEC's West Division and landed in the NCAA Tournament.

That team was on a mission to gain some respect for the program. Even after they got off to a 10-3 start, though, the Rebels didn't get any recognition. Then third-ranked Kentucky came to Oxford.

More than 8,000 fans filled up Tad Smith Coliseum to see if their team was for real. Head coach Rob Evans thought so. He told his players exactly how they should tell the press

Rebels

"I told you so" after they won the game.

Sure enough, the Rebels won 73-69. They said just what their coach had told them to: "This was not a fluke. This team is for real."

Ole Miss was in the Top 20 the next week.

One day Jesus is going to come back and find everyone who has been faithful to him. He will gather them all up and take them to Heaven. There they will live with God forever in happiness and love. It will be the most glorious time ever.

How do we know that's going to happen? Jesus told us so. When will it happen? Well, he didn't tell us that. He just told us to be ready so we don't miss it.

How do you get ready? It's simple. You just love Jesus. You live your life for Jesus. You remember that Jesus is counting on you, and you do everything for him.

Are you ready?

Put some ice cream in a bowl and watch it melt to remind you that Jesus may come back at any time, maybe even before the ice cream melts.

Ole Miss

THE GAME OF LIFE

Read 1 Corinthians 9:24-27.

Run so you will get the prize.

Too bad for Nebraska they weren't playing a video game when they met the Rebels. Instead, the game was football.

As part of the fun before the 2002 Independence Bowl, Nebraska and Mississippi football players had a cyber showdown. They played a lot of video games against each other. Sadly, the Cornhuskers creamed the Rebels.

But that was just for fun. The football game was the real deal. On the field, the Ole Miss defense completely controlled the Huskers.

In fact, the defense turned the game around with a big play. Nebraska led 10-0 early when Von Hutchins intercepted a pass. It was the kind of killer play the Huskers had made in the video games, the ones that didn't matter.

Quarterback Eli Manning threw a touchdown

pass six plays later, and the Huskers couldn't regain the momentum. Ole Miss won 27-23.

Life is often compared to a game, but what are the rules? Who sets them? How do you win? What's the prize if you do win?

Sometimes life doesn't seem to make any sense at all, does it? You just make it up as you go along. But what if that's because the greatest gamer of them all — God — is in charge? Life is his game; life has his rules.

God's rules for the game of life are spelled out in his book. The game has a purpose: You are alive to glorify God.

And so God's game has winners and losers. The winners are those who glorify God by finding their salvation in Jesus Christ. The losers are those who don't. The prize for winning the game of life is the grand prize: eternal life in Heaven with God.

Play ball.

Play a game: Give each family member thirty seconds to tell things God did for them today. The winner is the one who comes up with the most.

AS A RULE

Read Luke 5:27-32.

Some religious leaders complained because Jesus broke the rules and ate with sinners.

An Ole Miss player once did something so shocking a rule was passed to keep him from doing it again.

Even into the 1920s, the rules about football uniforms were rather loose. Reb back Claude "Tadpole" Smith wouldn't wear a helmet. He said it slowed him down. Smith also taped his ears back to reduce wind resistance.

The Rebels beat Florida 12-7 in 1927. The winning touchdown came on a pass caught by team captain Austin Applewhite. It was during this game that he did something that brought about a change in the rules.

What awful thing did he do? In that Florida heat, he took his jersey off during the game.

Rebels

The Florida coach complained, and the ref told Applewhite to put his jersey back on. The Rebel leader said if the ref could find it in the rule book, he'd do it. There was no such rule.

So Applewhite scored the game-winning touchdown without a shirt.

You live with a whole set of rules, don't you? Go to bed at a certain time. Don't play in the street. Don't act ugly to your brother or sister. Be polite to your teachers.

Rules are hard but they aren't always bad things. Without them, our whole world and our country would be a mess. Nobody would get along, and people couldn't do stuff together.

The rules Jesus didn't like were those that said some people should be treated badly. He broke them, and he expects you to do it, too. You should never mistreat anybody just because somebody says it's the thing to do.

Jesus loves that person. So should you.

Think of a rule that you don't like.
Why do you think you have it?
What would happen if you broke it?

Ole Miss

TIRED OUT

Read Matthew 11:27-30.

Jesus said, "Come to me and I will give you rest."

An Ole Miss football player was once so tired he went off the field on the wrong side so he wouldn't have to go back into the game.

The 1948 team rolled to an 8-1 record. The star was three-time All-American end Barney Poole. Because he played for Army during World War II, he played seven years of college football. In the Tulane game in '48, Poole was hit so hard by a tackler that it knocked out eight teeth. He missed only two plays.

The Rebs whipped LSU that season 49-19. Seven different players scored touchdowns. One who didn't was running back Billy Mustin. The quarterback kept giving him the ball so he could score a touchdown. "Every time we got close, [the quarterback] would give the ball to me," Mustin recalled. "It was wearing me out."

Finally, Mustin had had enough. He got to his feet after a run and trotted over to the LSU sideline. A Tiger manager said, "You're coming off the wrong side." A worn out Mustin told him, "If I go back over there, they are going to put me back in."

Don't you just get tired sometime? Maybe after a tough day at school when you stayed up too late the night before. Have you ever gotten so tired on a trip that you fell asleep in the back seat of the car?

Everybody gets tired, grown-ups and kids alike. And sometimes, like grown-ups, when you're tired, you have to just keep on going. You have to finish something you've started no matter how tired you are.

That's a good time to pray to Jesus. When you do that, you have the power of almighty God to help you and give you strength.

Talk about the last time you fell asleep in the car. Why were you so tired? Did you know God can give you strength?

Ole Miss

PRESSURE POINT

Read Matthew 26:36-39.

Jesus said, "My soul is sad. I feel close to death."

Because runners are side-by-side, track is one of the most pressure-packed sports of them all. Except in the case of one of the greatest Ole Miss runners ever.

Lee Ellis Moore ended his storied career in Oxford in June 2011. He was first-team All-SEC that year and was honored as the SEC's track-and-field scholar-athlete of the year. He won the SEC title in the 400-meter hurdles and was All-America.

Thus, Moore was so good that he ran with a bull's eye on his chest. Everybody wanted to beat him. But strangely enough, he never felt any pressure. That's because he never ran for himself or for his own glory. Instead, he ran for someone else's glory.

Rebels

"I run for the sake of the name of Christ and his glory," Moore explained. "I can say that I don't feel any pressure. I am not running to please men, but I seek to please my father in Heaven."

Even as a kid, you live every day with pressure. You must make good grades. You have to do your homework. You always have projects to finish and adults to keep happy.

Pressure can drive you to do your best. Or it can make you cry with fear. But God is right there to help you with the pressures of daily living. You pray. God will give you the grace to hang on and do your best if you ask. Just as he did Jesus when he faced the pressure of the death that waited for him.

Just remember. The most pressure of all lies in deciding where you will spend eternity. And you've taken care of that by deciding to follow Jesus. The pressure's off — forever.

Pray for God to help you. Then practice being under pressure by trying to say the alphabet in under seven seconds.

KEEP OUT!

Read Exodus 26:30-34.

The curtain will separate the Holy Room from the Most Holy Room.

He had to hitchhike to the game. When he got there, the gate guards wouldn't let him in. Yet, he was one of the game's defensive stars.

The Rebels of 1960 won their second straight national title. They opened the season with a 42-0 beatdown of Houston.

Junior guard Bill "Foggy" Basham didn't make the trip with the team because he wasn't on the traveling squad. So he hitchhiked to Houston and got to the game before halftime. A guard wouldn't let him through the gate; he just stood around outside the stadium.

By halftime, the Rebels were beat up and running short of linemen. The team doctor had seen Basham at the gate. He told head coach Johnny Vaught, "Foggy is here and wants to play." Desperate for players, Vaught agreed.

The player who had been kept out of the stadium emerged as a star the last half. Basham played "the finest 30 minutes of football in his life." He even caused and recovered a fumble on the second-half kickoff.

Like Foggy Basham in Houston that day, you know how it feels to be told to keep out. Your parents ask you to leave the room when they want to talk. Your sibling won't let you into his or her room. You're not sure you can get into a club at school you like.

You're not by yourself. The Hebrew people in the Bible knew about being told to keep out. Only the priests could enter God's presence and survive. Then along came Jesus to kick that barrier down and let you talk to God yourself. You do it through prayer.

Christianity is an exclusive club since only believers are allowed in. The catch is that an invitation to join is extended to everyone.

Write a note inviting a friend at school to your church; give it to him/her.

Ole Miss

BE BRAVE

Read 1 Corinthians 16:13-14.

Stand firm in the faith. Be brave.
Be strong.

The words on his grave are few, but they say much: "Chucky — Man of Courage."

In the 1989 game against Vanderbilt, Rebel Chucky Mullins made a routine tackle, but he didn't get up. He suffered four broken bones in his spine and was instantly paralyzed.

Reb head coach Billy Brewer said all Mullins could move "were his lips and his eyes, but they were always smiling. He kept fighting."

Chucky fought through 114 days in a hospital and four months in rehab. He couldn't use his arms or his legs, but he marched on. He kept going to classes and to football games.

Mullins' courageous fight ended in May 1991 when he died of lung problems. He was 21.

Today, Mullins' courage still inspires Rebel

players. Each season one player receives the Chucky Mullins Courage Award. Before each home game, the players touch a bust of Mullins as they exit the tunnel onto the field.

What do you think of when somebody tells you to be brave or have courage? Maybe a firefighter who runs into a burning house to rescue someone? Or a soldier who fights for our country so you can sleep safely at night?

They are brave people, all right, but you, too, show courage every day. Maybe by trying new things or by standing up for yourself with a bully.

God calls you to be brave every day by showing courage for Jesus. You stand firm in your faith no matter what someone else says. You tell others you believe in God and love Jesus no matter what.

If you do that, then to God you are a hero. Hey, how great is that?

Make a "courage box." Decorate it and put five slips of paper in it with ways you can show courage. Pull one out each day and show courage by doing it.

Ole Miss

TAKE A CHANCE

Read Matthew 4:18-22.

"Come. Follow me," Jesus said. They left their nets and followed him.

Ole Miss' second-ever football team took a really big chance — and got the school's first-ever upset.

The boys and their coach climbed aboard a train on Nov. 18, 1893, for the first road game in Ole Miss football history. The head coach wasn't all that sure about his squad's chances. "Every man realized that today he was going to be tested," he said.

The Oxford boys were headed to Memphis to play the Memphis Athletic Club, and they were big underdogs. The team featured a lot of grown men and former college players.

Back in Oxford, a group gathered at a local bookstore that had a telegraph. There they were able to receive news about the game. To their surprise, the news was all good.

Halfback Mordecai Jones, who scored the first touchdown in Ole Miss history, broke off a 60-yard touchdown run, and Ole Miss won 16-0. It was a chance worth taking.

Have you ever thought that you take chances every day? You risk getting hurt every time you play at PE, go swimming, or play paint ball. You risk getting a bad grade with every test you take. You still take chances, though, figuring whatever you get is worth it.

Simon Peter, Andrew, James, and John took a chance. A big one! They fished to make a living, and they gave that up to follow this wandering preacher they didn't even know.

Jesus wants you to take that same chance with your life by giving it to him. What have you got to lose? Nothing really. What have you got to gain? Everlasting life with God.

That's something worth taking a chance on.

Write a short story about Jesus coming by your house and calling you as he did the four fishermen.

UNEXPECTEDLY

Read Luke 2:1-7.

Mary gave birth to her first child. It was a boy she named Jesus.

The Ole Miss coaches had no idea what to expect. The Texas coaches knew exactly what to expect. So what happened was unexpected.

Head coach Hugh Freeze and his staff were caught by surprise when the Texas head coach fired his defensive coordinator the week of the game in 2013. "It's an unknown," Freeze said about getting ready to play the game.

The Texas coaches knew exactly what Ole Miss would do. Behind quarterback Bo Wallace and running back Jeff Scott, the Rebels ran the ball. "That's what we do," Wallace said.

The first half went just as expected. Texas' defense knew what was coming: the Ole Miss offense didn't. Texas led 23-17 at halftime.

In the last half, though, the Rebs knew what

to expect. They shut Texas down completely.

Even though they knew what to expect, the Longhorns couldn't stop the Rebels. Ole Miss kept running the ball and ran to a 44-23 win. A lot of folks didn't expect that.

Something is unexpected when you didn't know it was going to happen. It can be good or bad. Maybe you had a field trip planned at school and you woke up sick and couldn't go. Or you found a dollar bill on the sidewalk. Life surprises us a lot.

God is just like that. He surprises us so we can remember that he's still around. Like the time he was born as the baby Jesus.

God always desires to do something in your life. The only thing that holds God back is when you don't believe he can do something. Or when you don't live each day with God in your heart and on your mind.

You should always be ready for God to do something unexpected in your life.

Tell about a time you expected one thing and got something completely different. Was it a good or a bad surprise?

FAILING GRADE

Read Luke 22:54-60.

A girl said Peter was with Jesus. He answered, "I don't know him."

Barney Poole failed two college courses on purpose so he could play football for Ole Miss.

Poole is one of the Rebels' greatest players ever. He was a three-time All-American end who was inducted into the College Football Hall of Fame in 1974.

In 1947, though, he was still at West Point where he had played three seasons for Army. World War II was over now, so Ole Miss head coach Johnny Vaught figured it was time Poole came back home.

The problem was getting somebody onto the heavily guarded West Point campus. So the Ole Miss athletic director hired a big black limousine to look official. Sure enough, the guards waved them on in. They had no clue where they were going, but they happened to stumble up on Poole walking across campus.

He said he wanted to play for Ole Miss, but the Army head coach wouldn't let him go. So Poole decided to get out of West Point in a really strange way: He flunked two courses and was kicked out.

His awful grades in hand, Poole came home and helped the Rebels win their first SEC title.

We all fail at some things in our lives. That means we don't do as well as we expect. Maybe you crashed your bicycle one time when you rode it or didn't win a game at recess. Maybe you have failed a test or two.

Failure happens to everybody in life. Even Peter failed; he lied and said he had never met Jesus — three times! Yet Jesus picked him to begin the Christian church.

If we believe in Jesus, God always forgives us for failing just as he did Peter. The only failure that is forever is failing to love Jesus.

Think about a time you failed by doing something wrong. Did you ask God to forgive you?

GETTING EVEN

Read Matthew 5:38-45.

Jesus said to love those who don't like you and to pray for those who do you wrong.

The 1959 Rebels got a rare chance to get even, and they made the most of it.

Ole Miss was ranked No. 3, and LSU was ranked No. 1 when the teams met on Halloween night. It was one of the greatest college football games ever played. A late punt return for a touchdown carried LSU to a 7-3 win. "I've never seen a bunch of grown men cry like babies as I did that night in our dressing room," said Rebel quarterback Jake Gibbs. "Man, that game hurt."

But the Rebs won the rest of their games to finish 9-1, as did LSU. The Sugar Bowl set up a New Year's Day rematch. Ole Miss had a chance to get some payback.

Rebels

It was no contest. The Rebel defense held LSU to -15 yards rushing. Senior quarterback Bobby Franklin threw two touchdown passes.

Ole Miss coasted to a 21-0 win. Three polls named the Rebels national champions.

In a big rivalry like Ole Miss-LSU, one team is always looking to get even for getting beat the last time they played. It's part of what makes college football so much fun.

But real life doesn't work that way. Should you get even when somebody does something wrong to you? Jesus said not to.

The reason is that getting even with somebody only makes everything worse. It will make the other person want to pay you back and hurt you again. And so it keeps going. It's just a mess when you live like that.

Jesus said to do something much easier. Just forget it. Go on about your business. Go on with your life. It's more fun that way.

Talk to your parents about something wrong someone has done to you. What should you do about it?

FIGHT NIGHT

Read Hebrews 12:14-15.

Do all you can to live in peace with everyone.

A wild fight after a football game led to the creation of one of the most beautiful trophies in all of college football.

In 1926, Ole Miss beat Miss. A&M (State) 7-6. Despite a jammed toe, Ole Miss captain Webster Burke booted the extra point for the win, the only one he ever made in college.

Some happy Ole Miss fans rushed the field to pull down the goalposts. A&M fans didn't like the vandalism one bit. To save the goalposts, they went after the offending fans with their chairs. History records that the players from both teams just stood on the side and watched.

It's no surprise that the Ole Miss fans didn't take too kindly to getting clobbered over the head with chairs. Thus, the "Battle of Starkville" went on long after the game was over.

To prevent future violence, students came up with a football-shaped trophy to be presented to the winner after the game. Out of a nasty fight, the famous Golden Egg was born.

College football fans today don't break out into wild brawls the way they did in 1926. But have you ever played in a game of some kind where a player from the other team hurt you? Maybe you wanted to fight because of it.

No matter what happens, no matter where you are, no matter what someone else has done to you — fighting is never the answer.

It's not just because you make an enemy. It's also because Jesus said you should make peace and make a friend instead of fighting.

Trying to make peace isn't as easy as taking a swing or saying ugly things to someone. It does requires more courage than fighting. It's also exactly what Jesus would do.

Try talking to a person at school you don't get along with and making him or her your friend.

ONE-MAN ARMY

Read Revelation 19:11-16.

The armies of heaven were following him on white horses.

Fullback Arnold "Showboat" Boykin was a one-man army against Mississippi State in 1951. He did something that had never been done before in college football.

Boykin was hurt most of his time at Ole Miss. As a senior in 1951, he had scored only three touchdowns all season until the game against State on Dec. 1. In Starkville, the Rebels beat the daylights out of the Bulldogs 49-7. That was a surprise since most folks thought the game would be close.

Even more surprising was what Boykin did. He scored all seven of the Ole Miss touchdowns! Nobody had ever before scored that many touchdowns in a single college game. His 42 points set an all-time record for a game.

Rebels

But here's something kind of strange. All seven of Boykin's touchdowns came on the same play: a simple handoff from quarterback Jimmy Lear! State just never could stop Ole Miss' one-man army.

Do you picture Jesus as a gentle man who heals sick people and loves children?

That's how he was the first time around. But the Bible tells us Jesus will come back one day and he will look and act a whole lot different. He will be a warrior and will lead an army.

What will Jesus do at the head of his army? He will destroy all the bad people in this world, those who hurt others, who don't believe in him, and who curse the name of God.

It sounds scary and it is — but not if you believe Jesus is God's son and the Lord of all.

Think about this. For now — and until Jesus comes back — you're a soldier in Jesus' army. You can help conquer the world for Jesus.

Read Revelation 19:11-16 again. Then draw a picture of how Jesus looks as the Bible describes him there.

Ole Miss

PARTY TIME

Read Exodus 14:26-31; 15:19-21.

Miriam took a tambourine. The women followed her and danced.

The Alabama Crimson Tide threw a great big old party. They just invited the wrong guests to their shebang.

On Oct. 8, 1988, the 12th-ranked Tide and their fans celebrated the grand opening of the Bear Bryant Museum. Ole Miss was the guest at the party. The Rebels were supposed to add to the fun by rolling over and losing. Instead, they were very rude guests.

For a while, it looked as though the Bama football team had showed up late for its own party. The first half was scoreless, but then the Tide took a 12-0 in the third quarter.

From then on, Rebel tailback Shawn Sykes turned into a first-class party pooper. First, he ripped off a 53-yard touchdown run. Then

Rebels

with only 46 seconds left in the game, he ran right up the middle for a 12-yard score. Ole Miss led 15-12.

After a fumble, the Rebels scored again to win 22-12. Turn out the lights; everybody go home. This party was over and done with.

Man, parties are fun, aren't they? A birthday party with cake and ice cream. A swimming party. Remember that Christmas is a birthday party: It's Jesus' birthday.

It would be nice if life were nothing but one big party. Jesus can do that for you. With him in your heart, every day can be a celebration of the good life.

You will cry; you will hurt. You know that already, don't you? Life is just sad sometimes.

But Jesus lets you find joy in those hurtful times. You live knowing that the part of you where Jesus lives will never hurt.

If you make your life a celebration of Jesus and with Jesus, then the party never stops.

Ask your parents if you can have a small thank-you-Jesus party with three friends. Be sure to say a blessing.

Ole Miss

PRACTICE SESSION

Read 2 Peter 1:5-7, 10-11.

If you do everything I have said,
you will never trip and fall.

Practice makes perfect, or so folks have always said. That sure didn't apply to Ole Miss guard/forward Ken Turner.

Turner played basketball for the Rebs from 1967-69. He was third-team All-SEC in 1969.

Turner played during the Pete Maravich era. That meant, like everybody else in the SEC then, he played in Pete's shadow. On March 1, 1969, though, in the last home game of the season, he stole the show from Maravich.

Oh, the Pistol had a pretty good game; he scored 49 points. But in the closing seconds, Turner, and not Pete, made the difference.

With the game tied at 76, the Rebs turned to Turner. With two seconds left, he hit the game's last shot for the 78-76 win. He led the

Rebels in scoring with 28 points.

There was something unusual about how good Turner was that night. He had been sick all week and hadn't practiced a lick, not once.

Following Jesus means you do your best to live the way he wants you to. It isn't easy; you have to practice it every day just like you practice football, the drums, soccer, or a school play.

How do you practice being a Christian? Not by sitting in church and talking to a friend or playing a video game the whole time. Not even by just showing up to be baptized.

You help people, you read the Bible, you give thanks to God, you treat others the way you want to be treated, you pray, you tell others about Jesus, and, yes, you go to church.

And you practice these things every day, all the time. You do them until being like Jesus becomes just as natural as breathing, walking, and eating a candy bar.

Right now, make a list of the ways you practiced being a Christian today.

Ole Miss

LIVE ACTION

Read James 2:14-17.

Faith without action is dead.

Tennessee talked. Ole Miss played ball.

As strange as it may sound, Ole Miss' battle against Tennessee in 1969 began in August. That's when a UT linebacker said that he didn't think quarterback Archie Manning's arm was very much to brag about. He called the Rebels a bunch of mules.

Those words wound up stuck all over the walls of the Ole Miss dressing room. The week of the game on Nov. 1, the Ole Miss campus and the whole state were in a frenzy. A mule showed up on campus that week; it wore a sign that said, "Squeeze the Orange."

Then came the game, and the third-ranked Volunteers learned that talk without action is worthless.

The Rebs took the opening kickoff and went

right downfield to score. It was easy after that. Ole Miss led 21-0 after the first quarter and went on to win 38-0.

Only after the game did the Rebels do their talking. Manning declared that Ole Miss had proved it was pretty good at every position.

Talk is cheap. By itself, it just isn't worth too much. How much fun is it to sit around and listen to somebody talk? You get all squirmy because you want to get up and do something.

It's that way in your faith life. In church, you may like singing songs and watching baptisms. But sitting through a sermon is really hard sometimes, isn't it?

Even Jesus didn't just talk. He almost never was still. He constantly moved from one place to another, healing and helping people.

Just talking about your faith doesn't really show it. You show that Jesus is alive by making your faith alive. You act. You do kind things for people like Jesus did.

List some things you can do tomorrow to show that your faith is alive. Do them.

Ole Miss

THE NEW YOU

Read 2 Corinthians 5:15-18.

The moment you believe in Christ, you are a new person.

Senquez Golson was such a lousy football player head coach Hugh Freeze tried to run him off. Then he changed and became one of Ole Miss' greatest players ever.

"He didn't buy in and didn't know how to work," Freeze said of Golson. That all changed before the 2014 season. That's when Golson realized he had to change and start taking football seriously if he was going to succeed.

He drank only water and some juices. He quit eating late at night and gave up McDonald's. He started grilling protein at home and got his weight down to 176 pounds.

The result was an amazing senior season in which Golson led the SEC with nine interceptions. He was a first-team All-America.

He also made the most important play of the season. With 37 seconds left, he intercepted a pass in the end zone to seal the 23-17 win over Alabama. "I couldn't do anything but thank God,"he said. "It was unbelievable."

"I never thought he'd make it," Freeze said. But Golson did — by making himself over.

Have you ever seen one of those TV shows where they take someone, buy them some clothes, and redo their hair and makeup? It's called a makeover. It makes them look like a new person. But they're not a new person.

Those changes are just on the outside. When you get a haircut or get a new pair of jeans, you're still the same person, aren't you?

If you really want to be a new person, you have to change in the inside, in your heart. The way that is done is with Jesus. You become a new person when you do things to please Jesus and not other people.

List some ways you can change the way you look. Then list some ways you can change how you act with Jesus' help.

JUST PERFECT

Read Matthew 5:43-48.

Jesus said, "Be perfect, just as God is perfect."

The Rebels stood a chance only if they played perfect basketball. They did for ten minutes or so — and that was enough.

Carol Ross' Rebels were 22-10 when they met Maryland in the second round of the 2007 NCAA Tournament. Maryland was the defending champion and had beaten the Ole Miss women by 31 points earlier in the season.

Before the game, Ross told her team they would lose if they tried to play a perfect game. So Ole Miss went right out and ripped off a 10-minute span that was about as perfect as a basketball team could play.

Maryland led 6-2, and then "Mississippi put on a defensive display for the ages." The Rebs scored ten straight points. Even when Maryland scored, it made no difference. Ole Miss kept on rolling. With eight minutes left in the first half, the Rebels led 35-12.

After that perfect 33-6 run, Maryland could not recover. Ole Miss won 89-78.

Nobody's perfect. To be perfect means you never do anything wrong, you never make a mistake, you never do anything clumsy. Ever.

Oh, you can be perfect now and then. Like on a test. Or playing a song on an instrument. But you're not perfect all the time. Only one man was ever perfect. And that was Jesus.

But yet Jesus commands you to be perfect. Didn't we just say that was impossible? Has Jesus got it wrong?

Nope, not at all. When Jesus spoke of being perfect, he talked of loving perfectly as God does. To love perfectly is to love all others and not just those whom you like or who do nice things for you.

To love perfectly is to love everyone.

List three folks it's really hard for you to love. Then list something good about each one. Try to love them for that.

Ole Miss

A LONG SHOT

Read Matthew 9:9-10.

Jesus said, "Follow me," and Matthew got up and did it.

The Rebels were long shots against Texas Tech in the 1998 Independence Bowl because the whole football program was in a mess.

The season ended with three straight losses. The next day it got worse when the head coach left for Auburn. "Rebel fans were furious."

Assistant coach David Cutcliffe was named the new boss Rebel on Dec. 2. That didn't leave him much time to get his team ready for the game on Dec. 31.

Then the week before the game, Cutcliffe landed in the hospital. Doctors said he couldn't join the team in Shreveport; he was too sick.

There was more. Quarterback Romaro Miller was coming off a broken collarbone. Nobody knew how well he would play.

So there it was. All that chaos and a good Texas Tech team lay dead ahead.

How did it turn out? Cutcliffe made the trip, Miller set a bowl passing record, and the long shots won 35-18.

A long shot is someone or some team that doesn't stand a good chance of doing something. You're a pretty long shot to get married this year or to be named the Rebel head coach.

Matthew was a long shot to become one of Jesus' close friends. He was a tax collector, which meant he was pretty much a crook. He got rich by bullying and stealing from his own people, his own neighbors.

Yet, Jesus said only two words to this lowlife: "Follow me." And Matthew did it.

Like Matthew, we're all long shots to get to Heaven because we can't stand before God with pure, clean hearts. We have to do what Matthew did: Get up and follow Jesus. Then we become a sure thing.

Name five long shots in your life (like driving a car today). Then name five sure shots (like going to bed tonight).

MAMA SAID

Read John 19:25-27.

Jesus' mother, Mary, stood near his cross.

Peria and John Jerry didn't have time for football — and then their mother stepped in.

On their Mississippi farm, the brothers had to feed the horses and the goats, bring in the hay, gather the eggs, and clean the barnyards. There was no time for something as useless as sports.

But Mama Jerry took over the chores to free the boys for football. Every night when Dad came home, he found the checklist for the chores complete. "While I was cutting the grass, I would go in and out of the house cooking," mama said.

Meanwhile, Peria and John were becoming stars. Once they entered high school, though, their secret came out. Dad didn't mind then.

Rebels

The boys grew big, strong, and tough from all that work that included tossing hay bales and wrestling pigs in the mud. They would laugh and get right up even when the wild horses they rode threw them into barbed wire.

They went on to star for the Rebels. Peria was an All-American defensive tackle drafted by the pros in 2009. John was an offensive guard who went to the NFL in 2010.

And it all started because of their mama.

Mamas do a lot for their kids, and they do it all out of love. Even when your mama tells you to do something you don't want to, she has a good reason. It's usually for your good.

Think about Jesus' mama for a minute. She loved her boy no matter what. When Mary stood near the cross, she was showing both love and courage. No matter how wrong it was, Jesus was condemned as an enemy of the Roman Empire. She could have been, too.

Love your mama like she loves you.

Make a list of the things your mama did for you today. Did you thank her? Do you thank God for her?

VIRTUAL REALITY

Read Habakkuk 1:2-4.

God, why do you put up with the wrong things people are doing?

Did a teacher of Latin and Greek who knew nothing about football really coach the first Ole Miss team to a 4-1 record? Well, things weren't quite what they seem.

The official records say Professor Alexander Bondurant was the first-ever Ole Miss head football coach. He did indeed lead the drive to start a team back in 1893. But when the students agreed to form a team, he knew he didn't know enough to teach them football.

So Bondurant sent out several letters asking for some help. W.S. Rhea of Memphis, who had played some football and loved the game, agreed to help. He took a train to Oxford. An hour after he showed up, he had the boys blocking and tackling.

Rebels

He stayed for a weekend before he went back home. He left Bondurant a set of instructions on how to practice for the first game. That happened on Nov. 11, 1893. It was a 56-0 stomping of Southwestern Baptist. It's odd but Rhea was one of the refs at that game.

On paper, a classics professor was the first coach. In reality, it was a man from Memphis.

You know, sometimes things just aren't what they seem. It's like a mirror in a fun house at the fair. Have you ever seen one of those? It makes you look all wacky and distorted.

It's that way with the world; it looks like nobody's in charge. We have wars everywhere. People hurt and kill other people. Children go to bed hungry at night. What's going on?

That's what Habakkuk asked God long ago, and God answered him. God said things aren't what they seem. He said he was in control and one day he would make everything all right.

We just have to trust and believe in God.

As Habakkuk did, name some things you'd like to see God change about this world. Pray for those changes.

GOOD OLD DAYS

Read Psalm 102:1-5.

Lord, my days disappear like smoke.

They were some good old days, those years from 1958-62 when the Ole Miss-LSU game was the biggest one in college football.

In those years, both teams were ranked in the top 10 in five of the six games played. (They met twice in 1959.) What had been a local SEC rivalry suddenly became "nail-biting, dramatic battles for national rankings, conference championships and bowl games."

"It was hard-nosed football," recalled Jake Gibbs, Ole Miss' quarterback from 1958-60. "But it was clean football, just a lot of fun. A lot of us are still friends today."

Rebel head coach Johnny Vaught sometimes used mind tricks to help his team get ready. One year, his young players were worried and nervous while they waited to take the field in LSU's Tiger Stadium with its loud fans.

The head coach told them they had as many fans at the game as the Tigers did. The players didn't buy it for a minute (since it wasn't true). But then Vaught turned his team loose at the same time as LSU ran onto the field. The fans went nuts. "See, boys," he said.

Oh, those were good old days.

College football is different today because time does not stand still. That means things change. When they do, you have memories, things you remember. What grade are you in now? Remember last year and some of the things you did? Remember your baptism?

You will always have those memories. God is always with you, too. Today may be one of those good old days you will remember someday, but you must share it with God. A true "good old day" is one God is a part of.

Make a list of things you can do to make God a part of your day (like saying a blessing). Try to do them all.

A GENTLE MAN

Read John 2:13-16.

Jesus made a whip out of cords and drove the animals and the money changers out of the temple.

An Ole Miss legend was a true gentleman on the field. He even warned a player before he knocked him out of a game and congratulated a player from the other team for throwing a touchdown pass.

Frank "Bruiser" Kinard is still sometimes called "the greatest tackle in football history." He played from 1935-37 and was a two-time All-America, Ole Miss' first.

Kinard was a true Southern gentleman. In one game, he was being held almost every play. He finally told the criminal, "Look. I'm small and I don't like to be held." The player didn't stop. A few plays later, he left the game, holding a bruised arm. He didn't return.

Rebels

In the 1936 game against Miss. State, a Bulldog came into the game late and threw a touchdown pass. Kinard went over to him and shook his hand, even though the game wasn't over. He explained that he had played high-school ball with the State player and was just glad he got to play. "I don't regret it," the gentleman said.

A gentleman like Frank Kinard is kind, polite, and nice to other people. He isn't mean to others and always tries to do the right thing. Jesus was also a gentleman and acted like one.

But as Jesus showed that day in the temple, being a gentleman doesn't mean you're weak. It means you stand up for what is right. At school, you protect those who are weaker than others, who are being bullied.

God is a gentleman, too. He could bully you and boss you around. Instead, he gently asks for your attention and waits for your answer.

Talk to your dad or granddad about how a gentleman acts. Decide if that is how God wants you to act.

Ole Miss

BEAUTIFUL PEOPLE

Read Matthew 23:27-28.

On the outside, you are beautiful.
On the inside, you are like a tomb,
full of rotten bones.

The 1967 Ole Miss freshman football players had a special reason to beat Mississippi State. They wanted to keep their good looks.

Back in those days, freshmen couldn't play with the varsity. The rookies lost to LSU but then beat Alabama and Vanderbilt. Vandy was undefeated and bragging about how good they were. Ole Miss beat them 80-8.

In those days, when the freshmen arrived on campus, the older guys would give them awful haircuts. Then right before the season started, they'd shave the heads of the young players. By the date of the State game the hair had grown back enough so a guy didn't feel too bad about asking a girl for a date.

Rebels

The varsity guys told the freshmen they'd shave their heads again if they lost to State. Not wanting to walk around campus anymore looking like total goobers, the freshmen rolled to a 49-7 win.

Judging people by their looks is about as silly as it comes. It doesn't tell you anything about a person. Does she use ugly words? Is he a Christian? Does he like tacos, dogs, or music? She may not even like Ole Miss!

Jesus warned us not to get too caught up in how somebody looks. Instead, you are to look at whether people are pretty on the inside. Are they kind? Are they loving? Do they tell the truth? Do they love God and Jesus?

This makes up the inner beauty that Jesus wants from you. Jesus isn't interested at all in whether you have hot new shoes or a pretty haircut or straight teeth. For Jesus, it's what's inside that counts.

Think of some friends. Did you use the way they looked or the way they acted to decide to be their friend?

WORKING HARD

Read Matthew 9:35-38.

There are only a few workers.

The first Ole Miss All-American volleyball player was so into work she had the whole team singing about it.

In 2011, middle blocker Regina Thomas was named the Rebs' first All-American (after 35 seasons). She was also first team All-SEC despite an injury that ended her season early. She is a really good athlete, but there is much more to her than just talent. She works.

When coach Joe Getzin first saw Thomas in high school, he was most impressed with her attitude. She "would do anything to win," he said. Especially if that "anything" was work.

Thomas' attitude about work spread to her teammates at Ole Miss. They joined her in singing while they practiced and played. "Work, work, all day long," they sang. Everyone on the team knew the tune.

Thomas said singing about work showed how hard the Rebels were willing to work to win. "We're weird, we know," she admitted. "But we work hard so we feel we deserve our own theme song."

When grown-ups talk about what they do for a living, they're talking about their job. Work is just a part of life.

How about you? Do you work hard or hardly work? Even now, you maybe can earn a little bit of pocket money by doing your chores or by helping your mom or your dad around the house or out in the yard.

There's another kind of work you can do right now and all your life. You can work for God. Jesus said there are only a few people willing to work for God. That's still true, even today. God needs more people to work for him. God needs you.

So what are you waiting for?

Come up with some ways you can work for God right now. Get to work.

Ole Miss

HOMELESS

Read Matthew 8:19-22.

Jesus said, "I have no place to call home with a bed to sleep in."

In 1913, the Ole Miss football team had one of the strangest schedules in football history. They were pretty much homeless.

In the early days, the school didn't give the football team much money. So to raise funds, the team had to play most of its games on the road. This was really true in 1913 when the team took a pair of ultimate road trips.

They began the season with a trip to Virginia to play three games in eight days. The Rebels played VMI, Virginia Tech three days later, and Virginia Medical four days later.

That was weird enough. But then the team ended the season with the strangest road trip in history. The Rebels played two games on the same day 384 miles apart!

Rebels

Head coach Bill Driver took the first team to Arkansas to play Ouachita Baptist. Captain Forrest McCall took the second team to Hattiesburg to play today's Southern Miss.

The Rebs got a win and a 0-0 tie that day.

You've probably seen them around. The guy with a beard, a backpack, and a sign at the interstate exit. A woman pushing a shopping cart loaded with bags of clothes. They're probably dirty and they smell bad.

They may be women and children running from somebody who beat them up. They may be military veterans haunted by what they saw in a war. They may be sick or injured workers.

They are the homeless. They have nowhere to live and nowhere to sleep at night.

But Jesus calls you to show them mercy, not to hate them. After all, you serve a Lord — your Jesus — who, like them, had no home.

The homeless, too, are God's children.

Talk to your parents about a way you can help a homeless person in your town. Then do it.

CELEBRATION TIME

Read Luke 15:8-10.

Heaven celebrates every time a sinner turns away from his sin.

The Rebels once celebrated a win by giving their head coach a bloody nose.

On Sept. 27, 2008, Ole Miss beat the No.-4 Florida Gators and Tim Tebow 31-30. Quarterback Jevan Snead threw two touchdown passes and ran for another score.

But sophomore end Kentrell Lockett pulled off a play that is part of Ole Miss legend. He blocked the extra point that would have tied the game.

The Ole Miss defense then stopped Florida on fourth and two feet at the Ole Miss 32 with about 40 seconds on the clock. Snead took a knee twice and the wild celebration began.

Much of the celebration was just fine. Some of the Rebs boogied with the band and made a lot of noise in the locker room.

The traditional soaking of the coach with the Gatorade needed some work, though. The excited players hit head coach Houston Nutt with the bucket instead of the Gatorade. He was left with a bloody nose.

Have you ever whooped and hollered when Ole Miss scored a touchdown? Or maybe you just smiled and felt good inside the first time you got a hit in a softball or a baseball game or scored a goal in a soccer game.

When we're happy about something that just happened or something that we did, we celebrate. We also celebrate special days, like your birthday or Easter Sunday.

Did you know God and the angels celebrate, too? They sing and shout and throw a party quite often. They celebrate every time someone accepts Jesus as their savior.

Just think. When you said "yes" to Jesus, you made the angels dance.

What did you do to celebrate your last birthday? Why does your family celebrate Christmas?

SMART MOVE

Read 1 Kings 4:29-31; 11:4.

> *Solomon was wise until he grew old and didn't follow God with all his heart anymore.*

Sean Tuohy made a smart move when he decided to play basketball for Ole Miss. Pretty girls helped make up his mind.

Tuohy is most famous now as the dad in *The Blind Side*. He is, though, one of the greatest basketball players in SEC history.

He was honored as an SEC Legend in 2006. In 1998, he was inducted into the Mississippi Athletic Hall of Fame.

From 1979-82 in Oxford, Tuohy handed out 830 assists. That's still the most in the history of SEC basketball. He was All-SEC three times.

Tuohy grew up in New Orleans, so why did he decide not to play for LSU? He had four reasons. "Ole Miss was horrible," he said. That meant he would get to play. LSU already had a point guard. He wanted to play in the SEC.

And then there was reason number four: girls. "Ole Miss had 1.2 girls to every guy," he said. That meant he had a good chance of getting a date now and then.

Remember that time you left your homework lying on your desk at home? That cold morning you went to school without a jacket? The time your library book was overdue?

Just because we make some good grades in school doesn't mean we don't do dumb things now and then. Plenty of smart people sometimes say and do things that aren't too smart. Like Solomon when he got old.

Some people even say that if you're really smart you can't believe in God. How dumb is that? Who do they think made us smart in the first place?

You got your brains and your smarts from God. Forgetting that isn't smart at all.

Think about this: If God didn't create everything, how did it get here?

HOW DISAPPOINTING!

Read Ezra 3:10-12.

Many older priests sobbed out loud.
They had seen the first temple.
Others shouted for joy.

The Ole Miss players were once so disappointed with their bowl trip that they said they wouldn't play because of some clothes.

The 1947 Rebels went 8-2 and won the program's first-ever SEC title. It was the best season in Ole Miss football to that point.

The team deserved a big bowl game such as the Orange or the Sugar. But here's something really strange.

In June before the season even began, the honchos from the Delta Bowl asked the Rebs to play in their first-ever game. They guaranteed Ole Miss $25,000. The Rebs accepted.

So the players watched in disappointment as SEC teams they had beaten landed the spots in the big bowls. Then the suit of clothes the players had been promised didn't show up. Several players told the bowl sponsors they weren't going to play without the suits.

Head coach Johnny Vaught put a quick halt to that foolishness. Disappointed or not, the Rebels whipped TCU 13-9.

Like grown-ups, you've been disappointed, haven't you? It happens when you expect something and don't get it. Or someone you know acts in a way you didn't expect them to.

The truth is that your parents, your grandparents, your friends at school, your teachers, your sisters and/or brothers — they will all disappoint you at some time. But don't be too mad at them. You will disappoint all of them sometime, too. It's part of being human.

When you are disappointed — and you will be — remember to keep your eyes on God. He is still good to you and still loves you.

God never disappoints.

Read Ezra 3:10-12 again.
Why were some priests crying?
How do you think God felt about that?

Ole Miss

BIG MISTAKE

Read Mark 14:66-72.

Peter remembered Jesus had said to him, "Three times you will say you don't know me." Peter cried.

One paper called it "the goof that laid the golden egg." A mistake helped the Rebels to a national championship.

The 1962 football team is the only one in Ole Miss history to go unbeaten and untied. The squad won the school's fifth SEC title and third national title.

The Rebels led Miss. State only 7-6 in the fourth quarter of the Egg Bowl. They needed a big play. What they got was a big mistake.

Quarterback Jim Weatherly faked a handoff to halfback Dave Jennings. He then went around his right end for a 43-yard touchdown that put the final of 13-6 on the scoreboard.

The play caught both State and the Rebels

by surprise. They had called a Jennings run in the huddle. But the handoff was botched, so Weatherly just kept the ball and took off.

One of the biggest plays of the greatest Ole Miss season ever was a mistake.

Only one perfect man — Jesus — has ever walked this Earth. Since you're not him, you will make mistakes. You will not make 100 on every test you take. You will not make every play in softball or soccer. You will trip and fall sometimes and embarrass yourself. You will be mean to others every now and then.

God will forget every one of your mistakes if you ask him for forgiveness. Even Peter's awful mistake in denying that he knew Jesus was forgiven because he came back to Jesus. He went on to be the main man in starting the Christian church.

The one mistake you must never make is to kick Jesus out of your life completely. God won't forget about that one.

What mistakes did you make today that hurt other people? Ask God for forgiveness of them.

Ole Miss

NAME IT

Read Exodus 3:13-15.

Moses asked God what his name was. God answered, "Tell them I AM *has sent you."*

One of the most important men in Ole Miss athletics had one of its coolest nicknames.

Claude M. Smith grew up "milking cows and playing with lightning bugs." One day at school, he fell into a ditch and crawled out covered with mud. A buddy took one look at him and gave him the nickname he would carry the rest of his life. "You look just like a tadpole," he said. Tadpole Smith it would be.

Tadpole spent the summer of 1925 driving railroad spikes in the heat. He decided that he wanted to go to college. A local attorney drove him to Oxford, and he never left.

Tadpole starred in football and baseball. He was later an assistant football coach and the head baseball coach for fifteen seasons. After World War II, he was the athletic director and led a huge drive to update the facilities.

In 1972, Rebel Coliseum was named after him. He is a member of both the state and the university sports halls of fame.

Nicknames like Tadpole Smith are often fun or funny names that say something about who that person is, on or off the field. First names can do the same thing; they can say a lot about a person to other people.

In the Bible, people's names reflect who they are, too. Biblical names show us a little something about that person's personality or how he or she acts.

The same works with the name of God. To know God's name is to know how he has shown himself to us.

As for you, what do you think your name says about you to God? Remember this: Just as you know God's name, he knows yours, too.

Have an adult help you look up the meaning of your first name. Does it match who you are and what you're like?

FEAR FACTOR

Read Matthew 14:25-31.

Jesus said, "Be brave. It is I. Don't be afraid."

Star fullback Charlie Flowers was afraid at least once during his playing days at Ole Miss — and he wasn't even on the field at the time.

As a senior, Flowers was an All-American in 1959. He led the SEC in scoring and finished fifth in the Heisman voting. He was inducted into the College Football Hall of Fame in 1997.

The '58 team went 8-2 and beat Florida 7-3 in the Gator Bowl. Quarterback Bobby Franklin was the game MVP. He didn't help the Rebels, though, when he accidentally kicked Flowers in the head in the first quarter.

The team doctor saw some blood and led the woozy star to the dressing room. After a few minutes, Franklin came to. When he heard cheering from the field, he raised himself up

on one elbow and shouted, "I'm going to die!"

The doctor said that wasn't so, but Franklin was still afraid he wasn't going to make it. "Why, Charlie?" the doctor asked.

Flowers said, "Well, Ole Miss is out there playing football and you're in here with me!"

Most everybody's afraid of snakes and big old hairy spiders. Lots of folks don't like bad weather, high places, or the dark.

Over and over in the Bible Jesus tells us not to be afraid. Does this mean not to fear a car that's coming at you? How about a big, slobbery dog that doesn't look too friendly?

Of course not. Fear is a helpful thing God put in you to help keep you safe.

What Jesus is talking about is being afraid of everything. Living in fear all the time. God says don't live like that. Trust in him, be brave, and he will calm your fears.

Think of two things you're afraid of. Are they things you should be afraid of or are they silly fears? Ask God to help you lose the fear of silly stuff.

Ole Miss

YOU NEVER KNOW

Read Exodus 3:7-12.

Moses asked God, "Who am I to go before Pharaoh?" God answered, "I will be with you."

Eli Manning wasn't interested in Ole Miss; Ole Miss wasn't much interested in him. But you never know what might happen.

The youngest Manning, of course, played quarterback for the Rebels from 2000-03. He set or tied 45 game, season, and career records. He was the SEC Player of the Year in 2003 and finished third in the Heisman voting.

Eli didn't want to be compared to his older brother, Peyton. So he told Tennessee's offensive coordinator, David Cutcliffe, he wasn't interested. That left Ole Miss as the logical choice, right? Not so fast, Twinkies breath.

The Ole Miss head coach was looking somewhere else for his quarterback of the future.

Rebels

Eli had decided on either Virginia or Texas.

But two weeks after Eli had told Tennessee no, Cutcliffe called him with news that changed everything. He had been named the head coach at Ole Miss, and he was on his way to the Manning home. He wanted Eli.

The rest is glorious Ole Miss football history.

You never know what's gonna happen in your life. Or what you can do until you try. You may think you can't play football, cook supper, or run the lawn mower. But have you tried?

Your parents or teachers sometimes tell you to do things you think you can't do. God is the same way. You just never know what God is going to ask you to do. Moses sure didn't. Can you sing a solo in church? Tell someone else about Jesus? Go on a mission trip?

You may think, "I can't do that." But if it's something God wants you to do, you can. You just have to trust him. With God's help, you can do it.

Think of something you've never tried before but would like to. Decide to do it and pray for God to help you.

IN THE KNOW

Read John 4:25-26, 39-42.

"We know that this man really is the Savior of the world."

The Rebels of 1952 pulled off one of the biggest wins in school history. They did it in part because they knew something.

That 1952 team went 8-0-2. The big game of the season was against third-ranked Maryland, which came to Oxford having won 22 straight games.

Head coach Johnny Vaught began preparing for the game before the season began by scouting the Terrapins. Then, as the game neared, he pulled out a projector in those days before video tape and digital equipment.

After watching the same film for hours, the coaches saw something. Just before the snap, the Maryland quarterback looked the opposite way he was going to run. The Rebel coaches also learned how the Maryland defense set up.

Vaught used that knowledge to draw up a game plan. The result was a 21-14 win that the press called the biggest upset in all of sports that year. The win also got Ole Miss a Sugar Bowl bid while the team was still celebrating in the locker room.

Just like the Ole Miss coaches knew something that day against Maryland, you know some things in your life. You know what your favorite subject is in school and what your favorite flavor of ice cream is. You know you're an Ole Miss fan.

Nobody can work it out on paper why you know these things. You just do. That's the way it is with your faith in Jesus. You know that he is God's son and is the savior of the world. You know it with all your heart and soul.

You just know it, and because you know him, Jesus knows you. That is all you really need to know.

List ten things you know for sure about yourself and your life. Shouldn't #1 be "I am a Christian"?

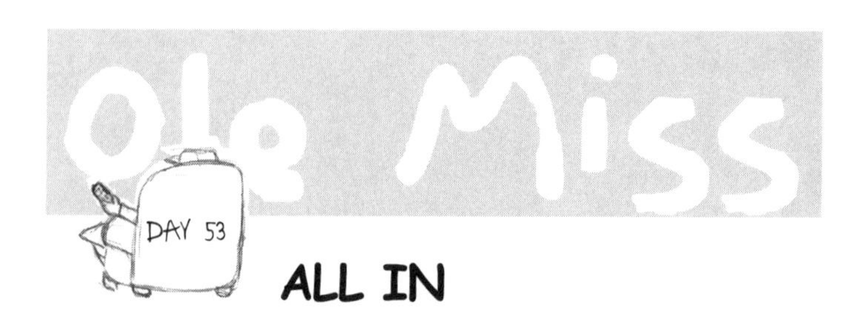

ALL IN

Read Mark 12:28-31.

Love the Lord your God with all your heart, all your soul, all your mind, and all your strength.

Once upon a time, football at Ole Miss almost disappeared because nobody cared about it.

After two successful seasons, the program ran into trouble in 1895. The students wanted more games on campus. The athletic association studied the situation but decided it was too broke to pay teams to come to Oxford.

Team manager William Cook had a real problem trying to round up eleven players for a team in 1895. The university magazine said, "No one seemed to care whether we had [a football team] or not."

But a few students did care. Cook managed to get his eleven players. He also scheduled a game against St. Thomas Hall, a high school team. It wasn't a real college game, but it did save Ole Miss football.

When the University won, students got fired up about football again. They held a big rally and raised enough money to keep the football program going.

What is it that you really like so much that you'd do it all the time if you could? It's called having "zeal" or "enthusiasm" for something. For instance, do you jump up and down and whoop and holler when the Rebels score?

What about your zeal for the Lord? On Sunday morning, if you go to church at all, do you pretty much act like you're getting your teeth cleaned or are about to get a shot?

Jesus made it clear which rule is number one to God. You are to be all in for God, to love him with all your heart, all your soul, all your mind, all your strength.

You should be fired up for God! Are you?

Promise God that at church Sunday you will sing real loud and will listen to the sermon and not talk all through it.

THE BIG TIME

Read Matthew 2:19-23.

Jesus lived in a town called Nazareth.

Jennifer Gillom's basketball career took her from a cow pasture to a palace.

Gillom grew up a long way from the big time: Abbeville, Miss., population 419, according to the 2010 census. When the kids played basketball, they didn't have a gym. They used what they had: a cow pasture.

"I'd go home very night and take a bath and it was black from the dirt," she remembered.

Gillom's journey to the big time really began when she showed up in Oxford in 1982. She ended her career at Ole Miss as the program's second-leading scorer. Her sister, Peggie is the all-time leader. As a senior, Jennifer was the SEC female athlete of the year and an All-American.

Rebels

She then went on to play pro basketball, get into the Women's Basketball Hall of Fame, and win a gold medal at the 1988 Olympics.

She completed her move to the palace in 2000 when the women's sports complex at Ole Miss was renamed the Gillom Sports Center to honor the Gillom sisters.

You probably live a long way from Washington, D.C., with all its big shots, or Hollywood, Calif., with all its movie stars.

Maybe you live in a small town nobody ever heard of. Or a city or the state capital. It makes no difference. Life is more than geography. It's about walking with God whether you're in the country or the city.

Jesus knew the truth of that. Think about it. He grew up in Nazareth. It was a small town in a region most folks never heard of in a little country nobody cared about.

Where you are doesn't matter. What you are does.

Get a U.S. map and figure out how far you live from Washington D.C. and Hollywood (Los Angeles).

TALK THE TALK

Read Mark 16:14-16.

Jesus told the disciples, "Go everywhere and preach the good news to everyone."

The Rebels once played a game in Cuba with a referee who confused everybody by speaking in both Spanish and English.

After the 1921 season, the Rebels played a game in Havana against the Cuban Athletic Club. The head coach gave each of his sixteen players 50 cents to spend on the train ride to New Orleans. "I took $8 to spend in Havana," said Ole Miss Hall-of-Famer Calvin Barbour.

The team took a ship out of New Orleans, and most of the players got sick. Once they arrived and got to feeling better, the Rebel boys had a grand old time. They were taken all over Havana.

The game wasn't that much fun as Ole Miss

Rebels

lost 14-0. The Rebs scored three touchdowns, "but they didn't let them count," Barbour said. "We were always holding or something."

The players were pretty confused since the referee gave his decisions in Spanish and in English. Nobody was sure they were the same.

You take it for granted that when you talk to somebody at school, they will understand you. Just think how awful it would be if your teachers didn't understand a word you said!

Now think about this. All over the world people speak different languages; they can't talk to each other. But billions of those people from all the countries of the world are giving their lives to Jesus. They are becoming Christians. How cool is that?

You see, everybody in the world has words for hope, love, joy, and God. And Jesus speaks those words better than anybody else — no matter what language is being spoken.

Learn the word for "hello" in three foreign languages. Then at school, walk up to three different people and say hello in one of them. See what happens.

Ole Miss

MUD WRESTLING

Read Isaiah 1:16-19.

Your sins may be bright red, but they will be as white as snow.

The field for the 1967 Egg Bowl was a mess. One writer said the last half was nothing more than "two quarters of mud wrestling."

The teams played in Starkville that year. At kickoff, half the field was under water and the other half was "a slippery, sloppy mess." A hard rain before the game turned into a shower that lasted all afternoon. All that rain turned the field into one big old mudhole.

After the first few plays, the team uniforms were so muddy that nobody could read the numbers. The Rebels' white jerseys were as dark as State's maroon ones.

The Rebels started out like they were playing on a sunny day. They scored ten points the first two times they had the ball. In all that mud, that was enough.

In the last half, the mud kept anybody from doing much of anything. Ole Miss won 10-3.

Everybody knows God made mud puddles to jump into and splash the water everywhere. And mud is really fun to play in unless you're trying to win a football game.

But with mud, you get dirty, downright filthy. You have to take a bath or shower to get clean.

It's like that when you sin, that is, do something God doesn't like. Like mud stains your clothes, sin stains your soul.

All Christians sin; so they all slip and fall into the spiritual mud. But they don't stay there. You take a spiritual bath by telling God you're sorry and asking him for forgiveness in Jesus' name.

Then as far as God is concerned, you're nice and clean again even when you're outside rolling around in the mud.

Take a bath or shower to wash your body clean. Then pray for forgiveness to wash your soul clean.

ALWAYS LOYAL

Read Matthew 6:19-21, 24.

Nobody can serve two masters at the same time.

In the Magnolia State, you must pick the team you follow: Ole Miss or Miss. State. Unless you're Breck Tyler, who did something no other player has ever done.

In 1968, Tyler was 10 years old and a big Ole Miss fan since his father was a Rebel assistant coach. "Mississippi State was the enemy," he said. He attended every practice and walked the Rebel sideline during games.

But when he was 16, his dad was the head coach in Starkville. He went on to play for the Bulldogs and his dad in 1977 and '78. Then his dad resigned, and Tyler did something that was really unusual. He transferred to Ole Miss and played for the Rebels in 1980 and '81.

Breck Tyler is believed to be the only player

in the modern era to play for both teams in the Egg Bowl. His office in downtown Jackson had a shelf with helmets from both schools sitting side by side on it.

To be loyal to something means you are faithful to it, always true, never giving up on it. That's what makes Breck Tyler's case so funny. He's loyal to both State and Ole Miss.

You are loyal to Ole Miss, but you are also loyal to God. God demands total loyalty, and that's hard sometimes. The world wants your loyalty, too. It wants you to act a certain way that you know God doesn't like.

A friend may use dirty words and tell you how cool it is. Other kids may go to movies that are not godly. You probably know kids at school who never go to church.

Jesus said you can't serve two masters. If you try, you'll love one and hate the other. So that means not being loyal to God means hating him. Your loyalty is to God — always.

Name some reasons you're loyal to Ole Miss. Think about this: Can a State fan say the same things about his team?

FUSSBUDGETS

Read Philippians 2:14-16.

Do everything without complaining or arguing.

Folks were fussing about the nickname of the Ole Miss football team. So they decided to get a new one.

The 1935 team went 9-3, and the fans were proud of it. But that nickname? Those same people started complaining about it.

What was it? Are you ready for this? The Flood. The Ole Miss Flood. Some folks called them the Red and Blue, but that was bad, too.

The sports editor of the campus newspaper set out to do something about it. He asked sports editors from around the South to help him search for a new name.

He wound up with more than six hundred suggestions. They included Raiders, Stonewalls, and Confederates. Ben Guider, an Ole

Miss graduate, suggested the Rebels.

In July 1936, the faculty committee on athletics — by a slim 4-3 vote — voted to let the football team be known forever as the Rebels. Nobody was complaining anymore.

This was one time fussing and complaining got something done. Usually, though, we complain — maybe even act ugly — when somebody does us wrong. It's a natural reaction. But Paul tells us not to. What's up with that?

Paul says that when you fuss, you're not acting the way Jesus would. Especially when you are real nasty to someone else. But if you don't complain, you're shining Jesus to that other person. God himself can brag about you to the angels in Heaven.

What should you do? Say a little prayer for patience and forget about it. You then walk away blameless before God. Now it's the other person who has something to complain about.

Before a mirror, pretend someone has done you wrong. Say a prayer for patience and watch yourself walk away.

GIVING UP

Read Numbers 13:25-28, 30-32.

Some men said, "We can't attack those people because they are bigger and stronger than we are."

A change in the rules and a bunch of babies led Johnny Vaught to think about quitting.

Vaught won 190 games, six SEC titles, and three national titles at Ole Miss. In 1949, his third season in Oxford, the rules changed to allow two-platoon football. Ole Miss wasn't ready. Vaught had always recruited the best athletes he could find, those who could play both offense and defense. But now the game called for one-way athletes who played either offense or defense. Ole Miss didn't have them.

And then there were the weddings and the babies. "Ole Miss players were having children by platoons," he said, and the coach didn't like it. The families hurt the team togetherness, he thought. So Vaught quit offering scholarships to married players.

When the Rebels went 9-10-1 in 1949 and '50, Vaught wound up depressed and thinking of leaving Oxford. But he didn't want to be a quitter. His grandmother wouldn't like it either.

So he stayed. The rest is Ole Miss glory.

Everybody feels like quitting at some time or another. Maybe football is harder than you thought it was. Maybe you just can't figure out math no matter how much you study. Maybe you and a friend just don't get along anymore.

Quitting is easy. But when it comes to God, remember the story of the people of Israel. They quit when the Promised Land was theirs for the taking. They forgot that God would never, ever give up on them.

God never quits on you either. So you must never give up on God even if it seems like your prayers aren't getting through. You just don't know what God may be up to. The only way to find out is to never quit on God.

Winners never quit; quitters never win. How does this apply to God and you?

LAUGH IT UP

Read Genesis 21:3-7.

Sarah said, "God has given me laughter, and others will laugh with me."

Coach Johnny Vaught once said laughter was part of what helped Ole Miss win. He had some stories to prove it.

Like the time a second-string back asked Vaught what time the team was arriving in New Orleans for the 1961 Sugar Bowl (which the Rebels won 14-6 over Rice). Vaught hadn't picked the traveling squad yet. He wasn't sure the player would make the trip. "What do you mean, we?" the coach asked. "Well, coach," the player answered, "you are going too, aren't you?" After Vaught quit laughing, he put the player on the traveling squad.

Then there was team doctor Ferrell "Doc" Varner. The players had a way of celebrating

Doc's birthday each year that made everybody laugh. They gave him $100 or so and then threw him fully clothed into the whirlpool.

Did Doc like it? Well, one year, the players gave him the money and forget the soaking. He stomped around the locker room until they remembered. They then threw him into the water while everyone laughed, especially Doc.

What makes you laugh? Is it someone at school who tells funny stories, makes funny faces, or can talk like a teacher? How about when milk comes out somebody's nose?

Adults don't laugh as much as kids do, but even kids don't laugh enough. It seems the world is just too serious.

We all need to remember as Sarah did that one of God's best gifts to us is laughter. The greatest gift of all is Jesus, and that's reason enough to laugh. Because of Jesus, you can laugh at the world's pain.

The tears you cry will pass. But your laughter, which comes from God, will remain forever.

Try to make somebody laugh by telling a joke or a funny story.

WELCOME HOME

Read 2 Corinthians 5:6-9.

We would really rather be out of our bodies and at home with God.

An Ole Miss All-American once traded a mansion for a jail cell — and was quite happy.

Barney Poole was an All-American end who played at Ole Miss in 1942, '47, and '48. He was named to the Ole Miss Team of the Century.

Poole grew up on a farm outside a small town. A basketball coach from Natchez saw him play once and went to Poole with an idea.

He told Poole he wanted him to come with him to Natchez and play football and basketball. He would find Poole a place to stay. So the youngster went.

It wasn't long before he was back home. He hadn't liked the place the coach had found for him. It was a mansion, and it was "too rich for my country blood," Poole said.

Rebels

The coach chased Poole down and told him he had another place. This one suited Poole just fine. It was a private cell in the local jail. "Got three good meals a day," Poole said.

When somebody says "home," what do you think about? A house? Your room? Your toys? Probably not a jail cell.

But home isn't just a place. More than walls and floors, a home is about people. You are at home when you are with the people you love and the people who love you. That's why it doesn't matter what you live in. What matters is the people you share it with, including God.

Oddly, as a Christian, you spend your whole life as a kid and as a grown-up away from your real home. That's because your real home is with God and Jesus in Heaven. There you will live forever with the people whom you love and who love you most of all.

You'll be home because you'll be with God, and nobody loves you more than God does.

List the different places you have lived.
What was different about each one?
What made them all feel like home?

Ole Miss

UNBELIEVABLE!

Read Hebrews 3:12-14.

Do not have an unbelieving heart that turns you away from God.

It's still hard to believe what the Rebels did in the 1971 Egg Bowl.

The Rebs went 10-2 that season and beat Georgia Tech 41-18 in the Peach Bowl. And then there was the Egg Bowl.

For three quarters, the two teams slugged it out. Ole Miss had a 6-0 edge on two field goals. But then there was that other quarter.

The game was 0-0 after the first quarter. Then in 9:27 of the second quarter came what one newspaper called football madness. In that stretch, the Rebels scored — get this now — 42 points on six touchdowns.

The first touchdown came after a short Bulldog punt. Fourteen seconds later, the score was 14-0 after a fumble and a run on the first play. Two plays later came another fumble and then a 28-yard touchdown pass. 21-0.

Then came drives of 60 yards and 3 yards. That last one came after another fumble. Then came an interception return for a TD. 42-0.

Who knows how much the Rebs might have scored if the clock hadn't run out 75 seconds later to end that unbelievable six-TD quarter?

It doesn't really matter if you don't believe in some things. Like magic. Or that walking under a ladder can bring you bad luck.

But it matters a whole lot that you believe in Jesus as the Son of God. Some people say that Jesus was a good man and a good teacher and that's all.

They are wrong, and their unbelief is bad for them. God doesn't fool around with people who don't believe in Jesus as their Savior. He locks them out of Heaven forever.

Believing in Jesus is about the way you live now and the way you will live forever.

Talk to your parents about some things you don't believe in and some things you do believe in and why.

DEAD WRONG

Read Matthew 26:14-16; 27:1-5.

Judas was ashamed and sad because he had betrayed Jesus.

Kentucky's head coach said no bunch of freshmen could beat his team. A ref signaled touchdown. A writer sent out a story that said UK beat Ole Miss. They were all wrong.

Johnny Vaught's Rebs of 1951 were a young team. They had only 21 players who had seen any playing time at all. Thus, Vaught had to put a lot of freshmen on the field, which led the Kentucky coach to say there was no way they could beat him. After all, his Wildcats were 20-point favorites.

Fired up by the coach's comments, the baby Rebels took the game down to the last play. Kentucky threw a pass into the end zone, and an official signaled touchdown. Up in the press box, a sportswriter sent out a news story that said Kentucky had won 23-21.

But just as the ball arrived in the end zone, Rebel linebacker Pete Mangum blasted the receiver. That blow knocked the ball out.

The Kentucky head coach was wrong. The referee was wrong. The writer was wrong.

The bunch of freshman Rebs had won 21-17.

Everybody's wrong at some time or other. Maybe you walked into the wrong classroom at school. How many times have you come up with the wrong answer on a test?

Here's a secret: Even grown-ups are wrong.

Think about Judas. He turned Jesus over to folks who wanted to kill him. Can anything be more wrong than that?

Judas felt sorry about what he did to Jesus, but it didn't help. That's because he tried to make it all right himself instead of asking God to forgive him. He was dead wrong this time.

When you do something wrong, you make it worse if you don't pray to God for forgiveness.

Think of something you did wrong today. Ask God to forgive you. How do you feel?

Ole Miss

FAITHFUL LIVES

Read Hebrews 11:1-3, 6.

Without faith, you can't please God.

Armintie Price wasn't interested in giving up her faith in Jesus Christ. She just wanted to ditch the skort.

Price is a Rebel basketball legend. She led the Rebs to the Elite Eight as a senior in 2007. She is the only guard in history to ever lead the SEC in rebounding. Only one other player in college history has done what she did: get 2,000 points, 1,000 rebounds, 400 assists, and 400 steals.

But Price had to get permission from her mother even to play basketball in high school. As part of the modesty required by the family's Pentecostal faith, Price couldn't wear pants or shorts. That included basketball shorts. So she wore a skort, a combination of skirt and short. She even wore it when she ran track.

Rebels

But when she got ready to head to Oxford, Price told her mother, "I still love God. I want to be saved. But I don't want to wear a skort." Mama said okay.

In your life, you have faith in many things. Faith in people like your parents, your grandparents, and your teachers. Faith that the Rebels will win, that the family car will start, that doing the right thing is the way to live.

This is all great stuff. It makes you a great kid whom everybody likes. Someone people can count on. It makes life fun.

But nothing is as important in your life as what you believe about Jesus. To have faith in Jesus is to believe that he is the Son of God. It is to believe in his words of hope and salvation that are written in the Bible.

True faith in Jesus means more than just believing. You do what Armintie Price does; you live for Jesus. You do everything for Jesus.

Come up with three things you can do tomorrow that will show others your faith in Jesus. Do them.

Ole Miss

RUN FOR IT

Read John 20:1-10.

Peter and the other disciple ran to Jesus' tomb.

The first football coach at Ole Miss did something that shocked a few of Oxford's housewives. He had the team go for a run.

Dr. Alexander Lee Bondurant is the father of Ole Miss football. He organized the first team in 1893. At 6:30 one morning in the autumn, he gathered thirty would-be football players in the old gymnasium. Not a one of the school's 173 students had ever played the game.

The first thing the 28-year old professor did was lead the team on a four-mile run. Man, did that cause a ruckus in town! The sight of a group of young men "led by a professor scantily clad, running through the streets of the town" upset a lot of the housewives.

Not a single student finished the run. Ten

left what another professor called "Bondurant's fool football team."

The next morning twenty students came back. Senior law student Alfred Roudebush, the team's first captain, told Bondurant, "Professor, we will see the season through."

He took them on another four-mile run.

You probably do a lot of running. You run at recess and at PE. Spot a playground and you run to it without thinking. You run during a game, whether it's softball or basketball. You run a race to see who's the fastest.

But no matter how hard, how far, or how fast you run, you can never outrun God. He is always there with you. He wants you to run, too — right to Jesus. Life is like a long race, and the only way to win it is by running it step by step with Jesus.

Here's something odd. The best way to run to Jesus is to drop to your knees — and pray.

If it's not dark yet, go out and run around your house, picturing Jesus running with you all the way.

Ole Miss

THINGS CHANGE

Read Hebrews 13:5-8.

Jesus Christ is the same yesterday and today and forever.

What kind of crazy game was this?

The ball was shaped like a watermelon! Players could barely hold it and couldn't throw it. Fans ran onto the field in the middle of the game and got in the way of the players. Players had long hair for protection because they didn't wear helmets.

There were no scoreboards. The fields didn't have lights so the teams couldn't play after dark. The halves were as long as what the players wanted them to be. Sometimes they played until they got tired and decided to stop.

Teammates dragged the guy with the ball forward. Some players had handles sewn into their pants to get tossed down the field. One time a player hid on the sidelines in street clothes; that means he didn't have a uniform on. When the play started, he stepped onto the field and caught a pass.

What silly game was that? Believe it or not, it was college football at Ole Miss and the South back in the early days. The game has sure changed, hasn't it?

Just like football, the world around you is always changing. You might get a new teacher or move to a new school. Your parents may get a new car for the family. You may even get a new brother or sister!

You change too. Your feet get bigger so you get new shoes. You may have grown an inch or two since last summer so you need new shirts and new jeans or skirts.

Even though lots of things change around you, there is one thing that doesn't change: Jesus. Jesus is the same all the time.

Jesus loves you always and his love for you never changes. No matter what.

What has changed in your life recently? Did you like it or did it scare you?

Ole Miss

THE FAME GAME

Read 1 Kings 10:23-25.

Solomon was so famous people all over the world wanted to meet him.

Ole Miss senior guard Bianca Thomas wasn't very famous — until the night she dropped 42 points on LSU.

It's not that Thomas wasn't really good. As a junior in 2009, she was first-team All-SEC. But folks must not have known her name very well. How else to explain the strange fact that she was a pick before the 2010 season for All-SEC *second* team?

"She's always been quiet," said Rebel assistant coach Armintie Price. She was trying to explain why Thomas wasn't more famous.

Then came the now-legendary LSU game. On Jan. 17, 2010, Thomas became just the fifteenth player in NCAA women's basketball history to score more than 40 points in a game.

Rebels

Her 42 points set a Tad Smith Coliseum record as the Rebels upset 12th-ranked LSU 80-71.

"I've never seen anything quite like that," said teammate Shantell Black of the game.

After that night, Thomas didn't have to worry about being famous. She led the SEC in scoring and was first-team All-SEC again. She was taken in the first round of the pro draft.

A lot of grown-ups want to be famous like the people on TV or in the movies. Fame just means that complete strangers know your name and face. Ole Miss football players are like that. A lot of people whom they've never met know their names and what they look like.

Are you famous? The answer may surprise you. The truth is that you are famous where it really counts. Members of the Rebel football team may not know you, but God does. God knows your name, what you look like and even what size shoe you wear. You are famous in Heaven where God and the angels live.

Name ten people you think are famous. Was Jesus on the list?

Ole Miss

MIRACLE PLAY

Read Matthew 12:38-40.

Jesus said, "Wicked and unfaithful people ask for miracles" to convince them he is Lord and Savior.

Even Ole Miss head coach Steve Sloan called the win a miracle.

The Rebels opened the 1981 season against Tulane. They dominated the first half and led 12-0, but a late touchdown was called back. Sloan said it took all the fire out of his team.

It did. Tulane dominated the last half and led 18-12. With only 2:13 left, the Rebs were in real trouble. They had the ball at their own 4, and they were without All-SEC quarterback John Fourcade. He had been injured.

One writer said, "All seemed very hopeless for Ole Miss." It would take a miracle for the Rebels to pull it out.

They got it. With just over a minute left, receiver Breck Tyler was supposed to run a short pass pattern, but he saw some open space. He looked at his quarterback and pointed over the middle. QB Kelly Powell saw it.

Tyler said it was the worst pattern he ever ran, but he caught the ball for a 39-yard score with 1:01 left. It ended a 96-yard drive. The PAT completed the miracle for a 19-18 win.

A miracle is something that you can't explain except by saying God did it. Some people say miracles are rare, but they are wrong.

Since God made the world and everything in it, the whole world is a miracle. You are a miracle! Just think: There's nobody else in the world like you. You're so special God made only one of you (unless you're a twin!).

A lot of people don't see miracles around them because they don't have any faith in God. Jesus knew that seeing a miracle doesn't make someone believe in him. But since you believe in Jesus and God, you can see miracles.

List some things around you that are miracles because God made them.

FAMILY TIES

Read Mark 3:31-35.

Jesus said, "Whoever does God's will is my family."

His family kept an All-American from playing football for LSU instead of Ole Miss.

Glynn Griffing was a first-team All-America in 1962 as a senior. He quarterbacked the Rebs to an undefeated season and the national title.

The problem for Ole Miss was that Griffing's school was closer to Baton Rouge than Oxford. "I really wanted to go to LSU," Griffing said.

The LSU head coach showed up at Griffing's home one morning, and his mother fed the coach breakfast. As he left, the coach told Griffing he had a bunk at LSU with his name on it. "I'll be there," Griffing answered.

He was excited about his decision, but his family sure wasn't. His dad told him, "If you are going to live in Mississippi, you ought to go to school in Mississippi."

His family's attitude turned Griffing's thinking around. He visited the Ole Miss campus and was impressed. He decided to play for the Rebels. This time, his family was happy.

Somebody once said that families are like fudge, mostly sweet with a few nuts. You can probably name your sweet kinfolks — and the nutty ones too.

You may not like it all the time, but you have a family. You can blame God for that. God loves the idea of family so much that he chose to live in one as a son, a brother, and a cousin. Jesus had a family.

But Jesus also had a new definition for what makes up a family. It's not just blood. It's a choice. Everybody who does God's will is a member of Jesus' family.

That includes you. You have family members all over the place who stand ready to love you because you're all part of God's big family.

With help from a parent or grandparent, draw your family tree.

WHAT YOU WEAR

Read Genesis 37:1-5.

His father made Joseph a pretty coat, and his brothers hated him.

Once upon a time, an Ole Miss coach was considered nuts because he wanted numbers on his team's jerseys.

Coach Bill Driver came down from Missouri in 1913 to head up the Rebel program. Before the game against Cumberland on Nov. 22, the coach said the teams should wear numbers on their jerseys. Cumberland said no, that the idea was silly. It also lost 7-0, which probably had nothing to do with numbered jerseys.

The idea wasn't a new one. The teams from the East such as Harvard and Yale refused to go along with the change. One writer said the schools came up with the ridiculous excuse that numbers on the jerseys made the sport look like a business. The Harvard coach also said numbers would make the players look like convicts.

Coach Driver won out, though. On Oct. 17, 1914, the Rebels defeated LSU in Baton Rouge. Both teams wore jerseys with numbers.

You dress a certain way for school and for church and to play in a football, softball, or soccer game. How silly would it be to wear shoes and a coat into a swimming pool?

Your clothes wear out and you outgrow them. So you change clothes all the time. Getting a new pair of shoes or some new jeans changes the way you look. It doesn't change you, does it? You're still the same person.

Do you think Jesus cares about the clothes you wear? What he cares about is your heart. What he cares about is how you act. It doesn't matter whether you're wearing clothes fit for a king or rags a homeless person might wear.

Clothes don't make you the person you are. Loving Jesus does.

Dress up in a wild outfit. In front of a mirror, act out what Jesus would say to you if he saw you.

NOTES

(by devotion number)

1 A bunch of young Baptists . . . people from Mississippi.: William W. Sorrels and Charles Cavagnaro, *Ole Miss Rebels* (Huntsville, Ala.: The Strode Publishers, Inc., 1976), p. 16.
1 For six weeks, a . . . by 10 each night.: Billy Watkins, *University of Mississippi Football Vault* (Atlanta: Whitman Publishing, LLC, 2009), p. 8.
1 Some Oxford folks . . . their own shoes.: Sorrels and Cavagnaro, p. 17.
1 had to pay their medical . . . and talked things over.: Watkins, pp. 9-10.
1 "Every man did his duty,": Sorrels and Cavagnaro, p. 17.
2 they scored 17 points with only 52 yards of offense.: William G. Barner, *The Egg Bowl* (Jackson: University Press of Mississippi, 2007), p. 250.
2 "went straight and long . . . Ole Miss fans went bananas.: Billy Watkins, "Rebels, Mother Nature Stop Bulldogs," *OleMissSports.com*, http://www.olemisssports.com/sports/m-footbl-spec-rel/112808aae.html.
2 the only field goal ever celebrated by both teams.: Barner, p. 251.
3 He came to Oxford . . . also as a Christian.: Janet Goreham, "Rebel with a Cause," *Sharing the Victory Magazine*, http://www.sharingthevictory.com/vsItemDisplay.lsp?method=display&objectid=Ad9A09.
4 The new head coach in . . . they looked like shorts.: Sorrels and Cavagnaro, p. 134.
4 Everybody quickly came to . . . up and down and cussed.: Sorrels and Cavagnaro, p. 135.
5 the Rebel sideline began . . . went in at right tackle.: Rick Cleveland, "Injuries? Noise? Pressure?" *Rebel Run* (Jackson: *The Clarion-Ledger*/Sports Publishing L.L.C., 2004), p. 119.
5 Quarterback Eli Manning had . . . do on some plays.: Michael Wallace, "6-0: Only One to Go," *Rebel Run* (Jackson: *The Clarion-Ledger*/Sports Publishing L.L.C., 2004), p. 120.
6 "I don't know if . . . The year was 1966.: Sorrels and Cavagnaro, p. 249.
6 "All I needed was . . . made up my mind.": Sorrels and Cavagnaro, p. 249.
7 She was swinging at . . . gave them to her.: David Brandt, "Grill's New Patience at Plate," *The Clarion-Ledger,* April 15, 2010, https://secure/pqarchiver.com/clarionledger/access/2009830301.html.
8 Rebel head coach Hugh . . . out of the game.: Austin Miller, "Wallace Cements Legacy," *olemisssports.com*, Nov. 29, 2014, http://www.scores.espn.go.com/ncf/recap?gamesid=400548324.
9 One referee had . . . the crowd noise.: Sorrels and Cavagnaro, p. 209.
9 Green's kick started . . . kick was good.: Sorrels and Cavagnaro, p. 210.
9 Almost everyone in . . . called it good.": Sorrels and Cavagnaro, p. 211.
10 We're going to win them all.": Sorrels and Cavagnaro, p. 190.
10 About two hundred . . . to win them all!": Sorrels and Cavagnaro, p. 190.
11 "Mom had black-eyed . . . watch the Cotton Bowl,": "Texas Tech, Ole Miss Meet," *Sporting News*, Jan. 1, 2009, http://aol.sportingnews.com/ncaa-football/story/2009-01-01/texas-tech-ole-miss-meet.
11 They did blackflips at . . . carrying oversized flags.: "Snead, McCluster Lead Ole Miss," *Sporting News*, Jan. 2, 2009. http://aol/sportingnews.com/caaa-football-story/2009-01-02-snead-mccluster-lead-ole-miss.
12 officials from what . . . one of its games.: Sorrels and Cavagnaro, p. 64.
12 Boomalacka, . . . rah, rah, rah!": Sorrels and Cavagnaro, pp. 59, 61.
13 Conerly had a sign . . . best way I can.": Sorrels and Cavagnaro, p. 152.
14 She gave up on . . . about to go in!": Parrish Alford, "McFerrin, a Former Tupelo High Star," *NEMS360.com*, Feb. 10, 2011, http://nems360.com/view/full_stop/11339451.article.
16 "It was very hard,": "Arkansas Fans Greet Nutt with Boos," *Sporting News*, Oct. 25, 2008, http://aol.sportingnews.com/ncaa-football/stor/2008-10-25/arkansas-fans-greet-nutt-boos.
16 One threw an empty . . . in their homes.: "Arkansas Fans Greet Nutt."

17 The new Rebel head . . . back to Georgia.: Sorrels and Cavagnaro, p. 126.
17 His first day on . . . than a minute.": Sorrels and Cavagnaro, p. 126.
18 a sportswriter said was impossible: Sorrels and Cavagnaro, p. 227.
18 He was LSU's fastest player: Sorrels and Cavagnaro, p. 227.
19 More than 8,000 fans . . . Top 20 the next week.: Kelli Anderson, "Rebels with a Cause," *Sports Illustrated*, Jan. 20, 1997, http://sportsillustrated.cnn.com/vault/article/magazine/MAG1009379/index.htm.
20 As part of the fun . . . creamed the Rebels.: Michael Wallace, "Rebels Rule in Real World," *The Clarion-Ledger*, Dec. 28, 2002, p. D1, https://secure.pqarchiver.com/clarionledger/access/1834566511.html.
21 Reb back Claude "Tadpole" . . . reduce wind resistance.: Sorrels and Cavagnaro, p. 86.
21 In that Florida heat, . . . There was no such rule.: Sorrels and Cavagnaro, p. 93.
22 In the Tulane game in . . . to put me back in.": Sorrels and Cavagnaro, pp. 159-60.
23 "I run for the sake . . . my father in Heaven.": Matt Sigler, "Moore Looks to Cap Successful Year," *The Daily Mississippian*, June 7, 2011, http://www.thedmonline.com/article/moore-looks-cap-successful-year-ncaa-championships.
24 Junior guard Bill "Foggy" . . . second-half kickoff.: Sorrels and Cavagnaro, pp. 208-09.
25 Reb head coach Billy . . . He kept fighting.": Rick Cleveland, "Chucky Mullins — 20 Years Later," *The Clarion-Ledger*, Sept. 30, 2009, http://blogs.clarionledger.com/um/2010/09/16/from-the-archives-chucky-mullins-legacy-at-ole-miss.
25 Chucky fought through . . . to football games.: Watkins, *Mississippi Football Vault*, p. 109.
26 The boys and their . . . to be tested,": Watkins, *Mississippi Football Vault*, p. 12.
26 The team featured a . . . former college players.: Sorrels and Cavagnaro, p. 20.
26 Back in Oxford, a . . . that had a telegraph.: Watkins, *Mississippi Football Vault*, p. 12.
27 Head coach Hugh Freeze . . . "That's what we do,": "Mississippi-Texas Preview," *ESPN.com*, Sept. 14, 2013, http://www.scores.espn.go.com/ncfpreview?gameid=332570251.
28 the Ole Miss athletic . . . and was kicked out.: Sorrels and Cavagnaro, pp. 142-43.
29 "I've never seen a . . . "Man, that game hurt.": Watkins, *Mississippi Football Vault*, p. 65.
30 Despite a jammed toe, . . . point for the win.: Barner, p. 74.
30 the only one he ever made in college.: Sorrels and Cavagnaro, p. 92.
30 Some happy Ole Miss . . . to pull down the goalposts.: Barner, p. 74.
30 A&M fans didn't like . . . with their chairs.: Barner, p. xix.
30 players from both teams just stood on the side and watched.: Barner, p. 74.
31 Boykin was hurt most . . . three touchdowns all season: Barner, p. 147.
31 all of Boykin's touchdowns . . . quarterback Jimmy Lear!: Sorrels and Cavagnaro, p. 171.
33 With two seconds left, he hit the game's last shot.: Lee Baker, "Turner Hits Clutcher," *Jackson Daily News*, March 1, 1969, http://www.ole misssports.com/sports/m-baskbl.spec-rel/021409aab.html.
33 He had been sick all week and hadn't practiced: Baker, "Turner Hits Clutcher."
34 OLe Miss' battle . . . much to brag about.: Watkins, *Mississippi Football Vault*, pp. 90-91.
34 He called the Rebels a bunch of mules.: Sorrels and Cavagnaro, p. 265.
34 the Ole Miss campus . . . "Squeeze the Orange.": Sorrels and Cavagnaro, p. 266.
34 Manning declared that . . . at every position.: Watkins, *Mississippi Football Vault*, p. 91.
35 Hugh Freeze tried to run him off.: Mark Schlabach, "Finally, These Rebels Have Reason to Yell," *ESPN.com*, Oct. 4, 2014. http://www.espn.go.com/blog/sec/post/_/id/90168/finally-these-rebels-have-reason-to-yell.
35 "He didn't buy in and didn't know how to work,": Schlabach, "Finally, These Rebels."
35 He drank only water . . . down to 176 pounds.: Edward Aschoff, "Senquez Golson's Long Road Well Worth It," *ESPN.com*, Oct. 17, 2014. http://www.espn.go.com/blog/sec/post/_/id/90792/senquez-golsons-long-road-well-worth-it.
35 "I couldn't do anything . . . he'd make it,": Schlabach, "Finally, These Rebels."
36 Before the game, Ross . . . play a perfect game.: Graham Hays, "Rebels Get Defensive, Knock Off Defending Champs," ESPN.com, March 20, 2007, http://sports.espn.go/ncw/ncaatourney07/columns/story?columnist=hays_graham.
36 "Mississippi put on a defensive display for the ages.": Hays, "Rebels Get Defensive."
37 doctors said he couldn't join the team;: Watkins, *Mississippi Football Vault*, p. 156.
38 On their Mississippi farm, . . . into barbed wire.: "Gigantic Jerrys Excel at Ole Miss," *Sporting News*, Oct. 18, 2007, http://aol.sportingnews.com/ncaa-football/story/2007-10-18/gigantic-jerrys-excel-ole-miss.

Ole Miss

39 He did indeed lead the . . . practice for the first game.: Sorrels and Cavagnaro, p. 19.
39 Rhea was one of the refs at that game.: Sorrels and Cavagnaro, p. 18.
40 "nail-biting, dramatic battles . . . "See, boys," he said.: Ron Higgins, "LSU vs. Ole Miss Always Matters," *SECNation*, Nov. 18, 2010, http://www.secdigitalnetwork.com/SECNation/SECTraditions/tabid/1073/Article/216143.
41 "the greatest tackle in football history.": Sorrels and Cavagnaro, p. 119.
41 he was being held . . . He didn't return.: Sorrels and Cavagnaro, p. 117.
41 In the 1936 game . . . "I don't regret it,": Sorrels and Cavagnaro, p. 119.
42 Vandy was undefeated and . . . if they lost to State.: Watkins, *Mississippi Football Vault*, pp. 80-81.
43 When coach Joe Getzin . . . our own theme song.": John Holt, "Volleyball's Thomas, an All-American," *The Daily Mississippian*, Sept. 21, 2010, http://www.thedmonline.com/article/volleyballs-thomas-all-american.
44 The team played two . . . to play today's Southern Miss.: Watkins, *Mississippi Football Vault*, p. 19.
45 Some of the Rebs boogied . . . left with a bloody nose.: "Smiles Linger as Mississippi Looks Ahead," *Sporting News*, Sept. 29, 2008, http://aol.sportingnews.com/ncaa-football/story/2008-09-29/smiles-linger-as-mississippi-looks-ahead-to-sc.
46 "Ole Miss was horrible,": . . . date now and then.: Ron Higgins, "Tuohy Can Still Dish," *SECNation*, Jan. 27, 2011, http://www.secdigitalnetwork.com/SECNation/SEC Traditions/tabid/1073/Article/219710.
47 In June before the . . . The Rebs accepted.: Watkins, *Mississippi Football Vault*, p. 51.
47 So the players watched . . . halt to that foolishness.: Sorrels and Cavagnaro, pp. 150-51.
48 One paper called it "the goof that laid the golden egg.": Barner, p. 177.
48 They had called a Jennings . . . the ball and took off.: Barner, p. 177.
49 Claude M. Smith grew up . . . just like a tadpole,": Sorrels and Cavagnaro, p. 86.
49 Tadpole spent the summer . . . drove him to Oxford,: Sorrels and Cavagnaro, p. 84.
50 he accidentally kicked Flowers . . . in here with me!" Sorrels and Cavagnaro, p. 201.
51 Eli didn't want to be . . . he wasn't interested.: Ian Thomsen, "Out of the Shadows," *Sports Illustrated*, Nov. 12, 2001, http://sportsillustrated.cnn.com/vault/article/magazine/MAG1024520/index.htm.
51 The Ole Miss head coach . . . to the Manning home.: Watkins, *Mississippi Football Vault*, p. 19.
52 Head coach Johnny Vaught . . . defense set up.: Sorrels and Cavagnaro, pp. 173-74.
52 the press called the . . . of sports that year.: Sorrels and Cavagnaro, p. 177.
53 The students wanted more . . . to come to Oxford.: Sorrels and Cavagnaro, p. 27.
53 Team manager William Cook . . . [a football team] or not.": Sorrels and Cavagnaro, pp. 36-37.
53 When the University won, . . . football program going.: Sorrels and Cavagnaro, p. 37.
54 When the kids played . . . black from the dirt,": Dan Fleser, "Gillom's Game Grew Up in Makeshift Setting," Knoxville News Sentinel, June 9, 2009, http://knoxnews.com/news/2009/jun/09/gillom-a-real-standout-in-her-field.
55 The head coach gave . . . they were the same.: Sorrels and Cavagnaro, pp. 78-79.
56 "two quarters of mud . . . as State's maroon ones.: Barner, pp. 192-93.
57 In 1968, Tyler was 10 . . . side by side on it.: Rusty Hampton, "For 'Rebulldog' Tyler, Rivalry Not Bitter," *The Clarion-Ledger*, Aug. 24, 2003, http://orig.clarionledger.com/news/sports/football2003tab/zrusty.html.
58 The same folks started . . . the Red and Blue: Sorrels and Cavagnaro, p. 107.
58 The sports editor of . . . six hundred suggestions.: Watkins, *Mississippi Football Vault*, p. 36.
58 They included Raiders . . . forever as the Rebels.: Sorrels and Cavagnaro, p. 109.
59 Vaught had recruited the . . . either offense or defense.: John Vaught, *Rebel Coach* (Memphis: Memphis State University Press, 1971), p. 72.
59 "Ole Miss players were . . . to married players.: Vaught, *Rebel Coach*, pp. 74-75.
59 When the Rebels went . . . wouldn't like it either.: Vaught, *Rebel Coach*, p. 72.
60 a second-string back . . . on the traveling squad.: Vaught, *Rebel Coach*, pp. 149-50.
60 The players had a way . . . laughed, especially Doc.: Vaught, *Rebel Coach*, p. 152.
61 A basketball coach from . . . good meals a day,": Francis J. Fitzgerald, ed., *Greatest Moments in Ole Miss Football History* (Birmingham: Epic Sports, 1999), p. 36.
62 one newspaper called football madness.: Barner, p. 207.

63 Kentucky's head coach said no bunch of freshman could beat his team.: Sorrels and Cavagnaro, p. 169.
63 They had only 21 . . . any playing time at all.: Sorrels and Cavagnaro, p. 163.
63 an official signaled touchdown. . . . Kentucky had won 23-31. Sorrels and Cavagnaro, p. 169.
64 Price had to get permission . . . Mama said okay.: Dick Patrick, "Price's Relentless Hustle Inspiring for Ole Miss," *USA Today*, March 14, 2007, http://www.usatoday.com/sports/college/womensbasketball/dayton/2007-03-13.
65 At 6:30 one morning . . . in the old gymnasium.: Sorrels and Cavagnaro, p. 11.
65 Not a one of . . . ever played the game.: Watkins, *Mississippi Football Vaul*t, p. 7.
65 The first thing the . . . on a four-mile run.: Sorrels and Cavagnaro, p. 11.
65 The sight of a group . . . lot of the housewives.: Sorrels and Cavagnaro, p. 13.
65 Not a single student . . . another four-mile run.: Sorrels and Cavagnaro, pp 11-12.
66 The material from this devotion is taken largely from the pages of Clyde Bolton's book *War Eagle: A Story of Auburn Football* (Huntsville, Al.: The Strode Publishers, 1973).
67 "She's always been quiet,": David Brandt, "No Doubting Rebels' Ignitable Thomas," *The Clarion-Ledger*, Jan. 21, 2010, https://secure.pqarchiver.com/clarionledger/access/1944271281.html.
67 "I've never seen anything quite like that,": Brandt, "No Doubting Rebels' Ignitable Thomas."
68 Even Ole Miss head coach . . . the win a miracle.: Rick Cleveland, "Comeback Victory for the Rebels," *The Clarion-Ledger*, Sept. 10, 2010, http://www.olemisssports.com/sports/m-footbl/spec-rel/091010aaa.html.
68 Sloan said it took all the fire out of his team.: Cleveland, "Comeback Victory."
68 "All seemed very hopeless for Ole Miss.": Cleveland, "Comeback Victory."
68 receiver Breck Tyler was . . . pattern he ever ran,: Cleveland, "Comeback Victory."
69 The problem for Ole Miss . . . and was impressed.: Vaught, *Rebel Coach*, p. 100.
70 Before the game against . . . Cumberland said no: Sorrels and Cavagnaro, p. 73.
70 the idea was silly.: Watkins, *Mississippi Football Vaul*t, p. 19.
70 The teams from the East . . . players look like convicts.: Sorrels and Cavagnaro, p. 73.
70 Both teams wore jerseys with numbers.: Watkins, *Mississippi Football Vaul*t, p. 20.

Ole Miss

WORKS USED

Alford, Parrish. "McFerrin, a Former Tupelo High Star, Lands Starting Role for Ole Miss." *NEMS360.com*. 10 Feb. 2011. http://nems360.com/view/full_stop/11339451/article.

Anderson, Kelli. "Rebels with a Cause." *Sports Illustrated*. 20 Jan. 1997. http://sportsillustrated.cnn.com/vault/article/magazine/MAG1009379/index.htm.

"Arkansas Fans Greet Nutt with Boos." *Sporting News*. 25 Oct. 25 2008. http://aol.sportingnews.com/ncaa-football/stor/2008-10-25/arkansas-fans-greet-nutt-boos.

Aschoff, Edward. "Senquez Golson's Long Road Well Worth It." *ESPN.com*. 17 Oct. 2014. http://www.espn.go.com/blog/sec/post/_/id/90792/senquez-golsons-long-road-well-worth-it.

Baker, Lee. "Turner Hits Clutcher as Rebs Nip Tigers." *Jackson Daily News*. 1 March 1969. http://www.ole misssports.com/sports/m-baskbl.spec-rel/021409aab.html.

Barner, William G. The Egg Bowl: Mississippi State vs. Ole Miss. Jackson: University Press of Mississippi, 2007.

Bolton Clyde. *War Eagle: A Story of Auburn Football*. Huntsville, Al.: The Strode Publishers, 1973.

Brandt, David. "Grill's New Patience at Plate May Lift UM to NCAA Bid." *The Clarion-Ledger*. 15 April 2010. https://scure/pqarchiver.com/clarionledger/access/2009830301.html.

-----. "No Doubting Rebels' Ignitable Thomas." *The Clarion-Ledger*. 21 Jan. 2010. https://secure.pqarchiver.com/clarionledger/access/1944271281.html.

Cleveland, Rick. "Chucky Mullins — 20 Years Later: What Is His Legacy?" *The Clarion-Ledger*. 30 Sept. 2009. http://blogs.clarionledger.com/um/2010/09/16/from-the-archives-chucky-mullins-legacy-at-ole-miss.

-----. "Comeback Victory for the Rebels in the Superdome in 1981." *The Clarion-Ledger*. 10 Sept. 2010. http://www.olemisssports.com/sports/m-footbl/spec-rel/091010aaa.html.

-----. "Injuries? Noise? Pressure? Rebels Answer the Call." *Rebel Run: Ole Miss' Magical Season of 2003*. Jackson: *The Clarion-Ledger*/Sports Publishing LLC, 2004. 118.

Fitzgerald, Francis, J. ed., *Greatest Moments in Ole Miss Football History*. Birmingham: Epic Sports, 1999.

Fleser, Dan. "Gillom's Game Grew Up in Makeshift Setting." *Knoxville News Sentinel*. 9 June 2009. http://knoxnews.com/news/2009/jun/09/gillom-a-real-standout-in-her-field.

"Gigantic Jerrys Excel at Ole Miss." *Sporting News*. 18 Oct. 2007. http://aol.sportingnews.com/ncaa-football/story/2007-10-18/gigantic-jerrys-excel-ole-miss.

Goreham, Janet. "Rebel with a Cause." *Sharing the Victory Magazine*. http://www.sharingthevictory.com/vsItemDisplay.lsp?method=display&objectid=AD9A09.

Hampton, Rusty. "For 'Rebulldog' Tyler, Rivalry Not Bitter." *The Clarion-Ledger*. 24 Aug. 2003. http://orig.clarionledger.com/news/sports/football2003tab/zrusty.html.

Hays, Graham. "Rebels Get Defensive, Knock Off Defending Champs." *ESPN.com*. 20 March 2007. http://sports.espn.go/ncw/ncaatourney07/columns/story?columnist=hays_graham.

Higgins, Ron. "LSU vs. Ole Miss Always Matters." *SECNation*. 18 Nov. 2010. http://www.secdigitalnetwork.com/SECNation/SECTraditions/tabid/1073/Article/216143.

-----. "Tuohy Can Still Dish." *SECNation*. 27 Jan. 2011. http://www.secdigitalnetwork.com/SECNation/SECTraditions/tabid/1073/Article/219710.

Holt, Holt. "Volleyball's Thomas, an All-American." *The Daily Mississippian*. 21 Sept. 2010. http://www.thedmonline.com/article/volleyballs-thomas-all-american.

Miller, Austin. "Wallace Cements Legacy with Gusty [*sic*] Performance." *olemisssports.com*. Nov. 29 2014, http://www.scores.espn.go.com/ncfrecap?gamesid=

400548324.
"Mississippi-Texas Preview." *ESPN.com*. 14 Sept. 2013. http://www.scores.espn.go.com/ncfpreview?gameid=332570251.
Patrick, Dick. "Price's Relentless Hustle Inspiring for Ole Miss." *USA Today*. 14 March 2007. http://www.usatoday.com/sports/college/womensbasketball/dayton/2007-03-13.
Schlabach, Mark. "Finally, These Rebels Have Reason to Yell." *ESPN.com*. 4 Oct. 2014. http://www.espn.go.com/blog/sec/post/_/id/90168/finally-these-rebels-have-reason-to-yell.
Sigler, Matt. "Moore Looks to Cap Successful Year." *The Daily Mississippian*. 7 June 2011. http://www.thedmonline.com/article/moore-looks-cap-successful-year-ncaa-championships.
"Snead, McCluster Lead Ole Miss Past Texas Tech." *Sporting News*. 2 Jan. 2009. http://aol/sportingnews.com/caaa-football-story/2009-01-02-snead-mccluster-lead-ole-miss.
"Smiles Linger as Mississippi Looks Ahead to S.C." *Sporting News*. 29 Sept. 29 2008. http://aol.sportingnews.com/ncaa-football/story/2008-09-29/smiles-linger-as-mississippi-looks-ahead-to-sc.
Sorrels, William W. and Charles Cavagnaro. *Ole Miss Rebels: Mississippi Football*. Huntsville, Ala.: The Strode Publishers, 1976.
"Texas Tech, Ole Miss Meet in Cotton Bowl Farewell." *Sporting News*. 1 Jan. 2009. http://aol.sportingnews.com/ncaa-football/story/2009-01-01/texas-tech-ole-miss-meet.
Thomsen, Ian. "Out of the Shadows." *Sports Illustrated*. 12 Nov. 2001. http://sports illustrated.cnn.com/vault/article/magazine/MAG1024520/index.htm.
Vaught, John. *Rebel Coach: My Football Family*. Memphis: Memphis State University Press, 1971.
Wallace, Michael. "6-0: Only One to Go: After 24-20 Victory, Just LSU Is Left in Ole Miss' Way." *Rebel Run: Ole Miss' Magical Season of 2003*. Jackson: *The Clarion-Ledger*/Sports Publishing L.L.C., 2004. 116, 119-20.
-----. "Rebels Rule in Real World." The Clarion-Ledger. 28 Dec. 2002. D1. https://secure.pqarchiver.com/clarionledger/access/1834566511.html.
Watkins, Billy. "Rebels, Mother Nature Stop Bulldogs." *OleMissSports.com*. http://www.olemisssports.com/sports/m-footbl/spec-rel/112808aae.html.
-----. *University of Mississippi Football Vault: The History of the Rebels*. Atlanta: Whitman Publishing, LLC, 2009.